Ella's kitchen

a tiny taste of the

Easy Family Cookbook

yummy + easy recipes
that big + little eaters will love

hamlyn

To families everywhere.
Whatever their shape, make-up
or size, family is family.
Love Paul, Alison,
Ella + Paddy

This special edition published
in Great Britain in 2017
by Hamlyn, a division of
Octopus Publishing Group Ltd,
Carmelite House,
50 Victoria Embankment,
London EC4Y 0DZ

www.octopusbooks.co.uk

An Hachette UK Company
www.hachette.co.uk

ISBN 9780600635376

A CIP catalogue record for this book is available
from the British Library

Typeset in Cooper Light and Ella's Kitchen®

Printed and bound in the Czech Republic

Created by Ella's Kitchen and Harris + Wilson

10 9 8 7 6 5 4 3 2

Recipe developer: Nicola Graimes
Photographer: Jonathan Cherry
Art direction, design + styling: Anita Mangan
Managing editor: Judy Barratt
Project manager for Ella's Kitchen: Angie Turner
Photoshoot direction: Sarah Ford + Manisha Patel
Recipe editor: Wendy Hobson
Assistant production manager: Lucy Carter
Design assistant: Ewa Lefmann
Illustrator: Shareef Ali
Jacket illustration: Havas Worldwide London
Home economists: Rosie Reynolds, Jayne Cross
+ Kitty Coles

Disclaimer

A few recipes include nuts, seeds and nut
derivatives. Nuts and seeds pose a choking risk for
young children – always chop or blend nuts and
seeds before serving, as appropriate to your child's
age. Anyone with a known nut allergy, or with a
family history of allergy, should consult their doctor
before giving nuts to their baby for the first time.

Honey should not be given to children under
the age of 12 months.

Take every care when cooking with and for
children. Neither the author, the contributors
nor the publisher can accept any liability for any
consequences arising from the use of this book,
or the information contained herein.

Publisher's notes

Standard level spoon measures are used:

1 tablespoon = one 15 ml spoon
1 teaspoon = one 5 ml spoon

Both metric and imperial measurements are given.
Use one set of measurements, not a mixture of both.

Ovens should be preheated to the specified
temperature. For fan-assisted ovens, follow the
manufacturer's instructions to adjust cooking times
and temperatures.

Medium-sized ingredients and pans and medium-
strength cheese are used throughout unless
specified. Herbs are fresh unless specified.

Use low-salt stock, and avoid adding salt to recipes.

Contents

Foreword by Ella's dad

When I think about family mealtimes, I see my young self with my parents and my brother around the same table; I see my own kids and my wife and the myriad occasions that we have sat together to eat. I think of those special occasions when, often with others, we have celebrated a birthday or an achievement.

Alison and I have always put the highest value on organizing our lives so that we can have as many family meals with Ella and Paddy as possible. Ella talks about the security of our Sunday pancakes routine, and Paddy enjoys getting involved in the day-to-day cooking. They have memories that hinge on family mealtime experiences – like the time we made a warming stew to eat outside in the February snow! And the time a trained cook came to Ella's birthday party and used garlic butter in the cookies. YUCK!

Ella and Paddy have become talented cooks, which I am sure is partly down to our family culture of offering them what we want to eat and of eating together. It hasn't always worked: I can think of meals they've walked away from having barely eaten a thing – but they survived! It's much easier to cook one meal for everyone and it's worth being brave. With that in mind, we hope this book will optimize both your own time and your quality family time. Alison, Ella, Paddy and I, along with the whole Ella's Kitchen gang, hope you enjoy using the recipes as much as we enjoyed creating them.

Keep smiling,

Paul

Paul, Ella's dad
Follow me on Twitter: @Paul_Lindley

4

Our easy family cookbook

A bit about using this book

At Ella's Kitchen we love it when families enjoy good food – from choosing what to cook and shopping for the ingredients to making the meal and spending time around the table – together. These shared experiences teach little ones that mealtimes are about more than just what they're eating. They learn that food creates social occasions during which we can share stories, connect with each other, and have fun! We believe that if children learn from a young age that good food is for everyone and that mealtimes are positive experiences, they'll go on to develop a healthy love of food that will last a lifetime.

Look out for our handy meal planner (page 64) – use it to help plan your week around the family table.

Feeding a family

We know, though, that it's not always practical for everyone to sit around the table to eat at the same time every day. As well as recipes that are good to eat together, we've included lots that we hope are brilliant for when you need to feed the kids an early tea, and keep portions back for the grown-ups to eat later. Every recipe tells you how many it's intended to feed (see icons, page 7). Serves 4, for example, approximates for two adults, one hungry older child and one toddler. However, every family and every appetite is different. You know your family best, so use your judgement and adjust the quantities to suit.

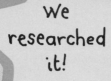

We researched it!

We commissioned the British Nutrition Foundation to review lots of studies about the best ways to help children develop a healthy relationship with food. The Foundation found that involving children in cooking, and eating together as a family can help to establish healthy eating habits. Encouraging children to explore and play with food using all their senses was also found to help.

Babies can join in, too!

Once weaning is established (that is, you've moved on from offering your baby simple veg or fruit purées), look for the recipes with the special bowl icons (see box, opposite), as these are recipes you can blend or mash just as they are to give to the littlest members of your family. Occasional pop-up boxes give you pointers on how to adapt other recipes for babies. Use your judgement when deciding what is suitable to feed your baby, and remember:

☺ Mash, blend or chop all food to the texture suitable for your baby's age and stage – adding a little cooking water or their usual milk, if necessary.

☺ Before your baby reaches six months old, avoid all dairy or other allergens, such as gluten, egg, soya and nuts.

☺ Until your baby is 12 months old, cook unpasteurized cheeses, including parmesan, and don't give him or her runny eggs or any honey.

☺ For older babies, even past 12 months, leave out nuts and seeds if you think they might pose a choking risk, or chop or grind them very finely until you're confident they're just right.

The best ingredients

All of our recipes have been approved by the Ella's Kitchen nutritionist. We've avoided adding extra salt or refined sugar, and instead we've used lots of herbs, spices and natural sweeteners (such as honey and maple syrup), to make sure everything is *reeeally* tasty, but also as good for you as it can possibly be. When we can't avoid using sugar (like in some of the treat recipes), we've always reduced the overall sugar content so that even the treats and cakes are better for you. Yippee!

We recommend that you use organic foods, especially for fresh ingredients. We believe that organic farmers produce their foods using the purest farming standards and that organic farming is better for the planet.

Finally, all the ingredients should be available in your local supermarket and you may even have lots of them in your cupboards already.

Key to icons

At the top of every recipe, you'll find a combination of the following symbols to help make feeding your family as easy as it can be.

makes
6 — How many pieces the recipe makes

serves
4 — How many family members the recipe serves

prep
10 minutes — How long the ingredients take to prepare

cook
10 minutes — How long the recipe takes to cook

freeze me — Whether the recipe (or part of it) is suitable for freezing

7+ 10+ — Baby age bowls: Suitable from 7 months old Suitable from 10 months old

Fun family mealtimes

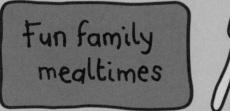

We all know that little ones pick up even the teeniest habits from us as they watch and learn. Eating together is a great way to embed some good eating practices – from the importance of munching on veggies and exploring food with all our senses to how to hold cutlery and to chew before swallowing! Here are our top tips for making sure family mealtimes are as fun and as positive as can be.

Research from Harvard University in the USA shows that the best way to boost a child's vocabulary is to talk to them at teatime.

Get everyone involved!

Learning to love food is not just about eating: getting little ones involved in buying, preparing and cooking it from an early age is important, too. Find your local pick-your-owns, visit local farmers' markets (marvel at the colours and smells, perhaps even have a few tasters), and use a trip to your supermarket as a voyage of discovery. The more you do together, the more your whole family will feel part of the foody gang, and so all-the-more excited about what you eat.

Cooking together is especially important. Even toddlers can help roll, weigh and stir, and lots more! Look out for our *Can I Help?* boxes throughout the book for other ideas on how to make cooking together part of your family time.

Keep feet on the ground!

Research suggests that if a little person's feet dangle, he or she will feel imbalanced and is more likely to fidget. If your little one's feet don't touch the floor at the table, pop a box underneath them as a foot rest, or come down to 'little' level and eat around the coffee or play table.

Inspire good little eaters

Lots of our Ella's Friends ask us how to help little ones learn to love a wider range of food. Here are our top tips:

☺ **Do nothing** When mealtimes become a battleground, they stop being fun. Tell any fussy eaters that it's fine to leave their meal, but they must still sit at the table with you while you eat yours. Hold your nerve – most little ones will start to nibble on something (and then gradually more and more) if only to pass the time…

☺ **Give little ones some control** If you're preparing a veg that can come several ways, allow them to choose which way (potatoes can be boiled, mashed or baked; carrots can be raw or cooked, and so on). Present veggies on a dish to allow self-service – offer three kinds with a deal that everyone must choose at least two to eat. (You can use leftovers in stews and sauces.)

☺ **Keep portion sizes small and appropriate** Little people have little tummies – an overloaded plate can feel off-putting. Offer small amounts with the option for more (and lots of praise) when it's all gone.

Make time!

Mealtimes may not always be able to include every member of your family, but try thinking of some creative ways to have more meals together than you do now. For example, if one of you works, could you all meet for lunch (a picnic is lovely) near the workplace? Could you have breakfast together – even if it means getting up 15 minutes earlier? If you can't have weekday family teatimes, are there evenings when just one of you could eat with the little ones? And, of course, earmark a time (probably at the weekend) when you all promise to eat a whole meal together. It might be Saturday supper or Sunday lunch, but whenever it is schedule that time as an appointment that you always do your best to keep.

No distractions!

Mealtimes are the perfect times to be together. Turn off the television, put away all smartphones and tablets, and make sure all little people have been to the toilet before you start. Talk about the food, engaging all the senses (what does it look like? How does it smell? How does it feel? What does it taste like?), talk about the day. Try to make sure everyone gets a turn to talk, respond and share.

Get-up-
and-go
brekkies

Palm tree porridge

serves 4 | prep 10 minutes | cook 10 minutes

Our quick-and-easy porridge has a dash of sunshine in the form of coconut milk and tasty tropical mango.

What you need

150 g/5½ oz **porridge oats**

600 ml/1 pint **coconut drinking milk**, plus extra to serve

½ teaspoon **ground cinnamon**, plus extra for sprinkling

1 **small mango**, peeled, stoned and cut into cubes

1 tablespoon **mixed seeds**, toasted

1 tablespoon **coconut flakes**, toasted

What to do

1. Put the oats, coconut drinking milk and 575 ml/18 fl oz water in a saucepan, stir, and bring to the boil over a medium heat. Stir in the cinnamon, then reduce the heat to low, part-cover with a lid and simmer for 8–10 minutes, stirring, until creamy.

2. If you are serving to young children, finely chop the mango, toasted seeds and coconut flakes.

3. Spoon the porridge into bowls and sprinkle with the extra cinnamon, the chopped mango, and the toasted seeds and coconut. Pour extra milk over the porridge, to serve.

Love your leftovers!

Turn any leftover porridge into a tasty snack: leave it to cool, then cut it into fingers and pan-fry in butter until golden and crisp on the outside. Lovely!

From 10 months

For babies

Leave out the seeds and mash up the mango. Remember to check the temperature before serving!

Spiced brekkie hash-up

serves **4** | prep **10** minutes | cook **20** minutes | freeze me 😊 **10+** (hash only)

A hash is a brilliant way to use up leftover potatoes and veggies. We love it for breakfast topped with an egg, and with a sprinkling of curry powder to make it tingle on the tongue!

What you need

3 tablespoons **sunflower oil**, plus extra for cooking eggs

500 g/1 lb 2 oz **cooked potatoes**, cubed

1 **onion**, sliced

250 g/9 oz **cooked sprouts**, halved or quartered, or **white cabbage**, finely shredded

2 **garlic** cloves, chopped

140 g/5 oz **halloumi cheese**, cubed

1 heaped teaspoon **mild curry powder**

1 teaspoon **cumin seeds** (optional)

4 **eggs** (optional)

What to do

1. Heat the oil in a large frying pan over a medium heat. Add the potatoes and onion and cook for 10 minutes, stirring often, until the onion has softened and the potatoes are light golden.

2. Add the sprouts or cabbage, garlic, halloumi, curry powder and cumin, if using, stir until combined, then cook for another 5 minutes, turning regularly, until everything is heated through.

3. If serving topped with a fried egg, put the hash in the oven (set to a low temperature) to keep warm, covering it with a plate to stop it drying out. Heat enough oil to cover the base of the frying pan and fry the eggs as you like them, then serve on top of the hash.

Just for fun

Around the world!

Herbs and spices are brilliant for a foody adventure. Gather together four spices and herbs with a distinctive smell – cumin, lemongrass, basil and cinnamon make a good start. What countries do they make you think of? (For these, we think India, Thailand, Italy and Morocco.) Show your little one where these places are on a map – food isn't from the supermarket, but all over the world!

15

Slurp-me-up smoothies

The green one

serves 4 · prep 5 minutes · freeze me

325 g/11½ oz cored **pineapple**, cut into chunks

1 small **avocado**, peeled, stoned and cut into chunks

2 **bananas**, sliced

2 handfuls of **baby spinach leaves**, tough stalks removed

450 ml/¾ pint **coconut drinking milk**

Blend all the ingredients together until smooth and creamy. Serve immediately.

If you like, you can freeze this smoothie to make a delicious, creamy ice.

The orange one

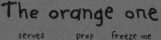

serves 4 · prep 5 minutes · freeze me
+ soaking

70 g/2½ oz unsulphured ready-to-eat **dried apricots**

Juice of 8 **oranges**

Juice of 1 small **lemon**

1 **carrot**, peeled and coarsely grated

Put the apricots in a bowl, cover with 125 ml/4 fl oz warm water and soak for 30 minutes, or overnight. Blend the apricots and soaking water with the orange and lemon juices and the carrot, until smooth. Serve immediately.

If you like, you can freeze this smoothie to make a delicious granita.

The purple one

serves 4 · prep 5 minutes · freeze me

300 g/10½ oz **strawberries**, hulled

40 g/1½ oz **porridge oats**

150 g/5½ oz **blueberries** or **raspberries**

1 teaspoon **ground cinnamon**

1 teaspoon **vanilla extract**

300 ml/½ pint **whole milk**

200 ml/7 fl oz **natural yogurt**

Blend all the ingredients together until smooth and creamy. Serve immediately.

If you like, you can freeze this smoothie to make a delicious yogurt ice.

The red one

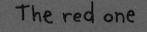

serves 4 · prep 5 minutes · freeze me

100 g/3½ oz **cooked beetroot** (not in vinegar)

200 g/7 oz **frozen stoned cherries**

1-cm/½-inch piece of **root ginger**, peeled and grated

450 ml/¾ pint **fresh apple juice** (not from concentrate)

Finely grated rind of 1 **orange**

Put all the ingredients in a blender and blend until smooth. Serve immediately.

If you like, you can freeze this smoothie to make a delicious granita.

Good-morning muesli bread

What better sunshine-y start to the day than with a special bread made of muesli and yogurt. Pressing the dough is a good way to get those muscles working in the morning, too!

What you need

Sunflower oil, for greasing

400 g/14 oz **wholemeal plain flour** (or 50:50 white and wholemeal), plus extra for dusting

70 g/2½ oz **sugar-free muesli**

2 teaspoons **mixed spice**

1 teaspoon **bicarbonate of soda**

1 teaspoon **salt**

115 g/4 oz **dried figs**, chopped into chunks, or **raisins**

300–350 ml/10–12 fl oz **natural yogurt**

1 tablespoon **lemon** juice

1 tablespoon **clear honey**

What to do

1. Preheat the oven to 200°C/400°F/Gas Mark 6. Lightly grease a large baking sheet with oil.

2. Mix the flour, muesli, mixed spice, bicarbonate of soda and salt in a large bowl. Stir in the figs or raisins, then make a well in the centre. Mix together the smaller amount of yogurt with the lemon juice and honey and pour the mixture into the dry ingredients. Stir with a fork and then mix with your hands to make a soft, sticky dough, adding more yogurt if needed. (Don't work the dough for too long as that will result in a heavy loaf.)

3. Tip the dough out onto a floured work surface and form into a round, then flatten the top until the dough is about 4 cm/1½ in thick.

4. Place the dough on the prepared baking sheet and sift over a little extra flour. Cut a deep cross through the dough almost to the bottom, then bake for 45–50 minutes, or until risen and the loaf sounds hollow when tapped underneath. Transfer to a wire rack to cool. Serve in slices. The bread will keep in an airtight container for up to three days.

Make me a baker!

Can I help?

This loaf is so super-quick and easy to make it's perfect for little hands who want to have a go at kneading.

Hearty red chicken soup

serves **4** | prep **10** minutes | cook **30** minutes | freeze me (soup only)

This is a big bowl of colourful wonderfulness! With crunchy sweetcorn, fill-me-up beans and a sprinkle of fajita spice, this extra-special chicken soup will satisfy your bellies, warm your toes and delight your taste buds.

What you need

1 tablespoon **olive oil**, plus extra for brushing

1 **onion**, finely chopped

1 **carrot**, peeled and diced

2 large **garlic** cloves, finely chopped

1 **red pepper**, deseeded and chopped

400 g/14 oz **passata**

500 ml/17 fl oz reduced-salt **chicken stock**

210 g/7½ oz can **kidney beans** in water, drained

½–1 teaspoon **fajita spice mix** (optional)

1 teaspoon **dried oregano**

250 g/9 oz skinless, boneless **chicken breasts**, cut into large bite-sized pieces

115 g/4 oz no-sugar, no-salt canned **sweetcorn**, drained, or kernels stripped from 1 cob

2 soft **corn tortillas**

What to do

1. Heat the oil in a large saucepan over a medium–low heat. Add the onion, carrot, garlic and red pepper, cover with a lid and cook for 10 minutes, stirring occasionally, until softened.

2. Preheat the oven to 180°C/350°F/Gas Mark 4. Add the passata, stock, beans, fajita spice mix, if using, and oregano to the pan and bring the mixture up to the boil. Reduce the heat to low, part-cover with a lid and simmer for 10 minutes.

3. Stir the chicken into the pan and cook for another 7 minutes, or until the chicken is cooked through, then add the sweetcorn and heat until the corn is warm and tender.

4. While the soup is cooking, make the tortilla chips. Brush both sides of each tortilla with olive oil, then cut into thin strips. Put the strips on a baking sheet and bake for 5–7 minutes, turning once, or until crisp. Transfer to a wire rack to cool. To serve, ladle the soup into bowls with the corn chips on the side.

From 10 months

For babies

Blend the soup with a hand blender, adding a splash of water if it's too thick. Slurrrp!

23

Salsa-on-top sweet potato

serves 4 | prep 10 minutes | cook 50 minutes

Baked sweet potato has all the fluffiness of regular baked potato with added natural sweetness and extra nutrients (the ones that give veggies their vibrant colours). We've heaped salmon and a fruity salsa on top of ours – irresistible!

What you need

- 3–4 **sweet potatoes**, depending on their size
- 2 cooked skinless, boneless **salmon fillets**, flaked into pieces

For the pineapple salsa

- 200 g/7 oz cored **pineapple**, cut into small chunks
- 1 large **spring onion**, finely chopped
- 4 heaped tablespoons chopped **mint**
- 1 small **courgette**, coarsely grated
- Juice of 1 **lime**
- ½ **red chilli**, deseeded and diced (optional)

What to do

1. Preheat the oven to 200°C/400°F/Gas Mark 6. Bake the sweet potatoes for 50 minutes, or until tender.

2. While the potatoes are cooking, mix together all the ingredients for the salsa. Adults may like to add the chilli to their portion.

3. To serve, slice through and open out the sweet potatoes. Flake the salmon over the top and finish with a large spoonful of the salsa.

For babies

From 10 months

Scoop out the flesh of the sweet potato and mash it down to the perfect texture with a little flaked salmon mixed in.

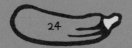

Surprise! Surprise! Cauliflower pizzette

The Italian word 'pizzette' means mini-pizzas, and our gluten-free mini-pizzas are super-special because we've used cauliflower to make the bases. Surprise!

What you need

Olive oil, for greasing and drizzling

90 g/3¼ oz **porridge oats**

1 **cauliflower**, cut into florets

100 g/3½ oz **ground almonds**

1 teaspoon **dried oregano**

2 **eggs**, lightly beaten

Your **favourite toppings**, such as slices of pepper and olive

125 g/4½ oz **mozzarella cheese**, drained, patted dry and torn into pieces

Freshly ground **black pepper**

Shavings of **Parmesan cheese** (optional), **basil leaves** and **mixed salad**, to serve

For the pizza sauce

200 g/7 oz **passata**

1 **garlic** clove, crushed

½ small **red pepper**, deseeded and sliced

1 tablespoon **tomato purée**

What to do

1. Preheat the oven to 220°C/425°F/Gas Mark 7. Line two large baking sheets with baking parchment and grease liberally with oil.

2. Process the oats to a powder in a food processor, then tip them into a bowl. Put the cauliflower in the processor and blitz until finely chopped to a crumb. Tip the cauliflower into the bowl with the oats and add the ground almonds, half the oregano and the eggs. Season with pepper and stir until combined – it will be fairly wet and crumbly but will hold together when baked.

3. Press the cauliflower mixture down into the bowl in an even layer. Scoop out a quarter of the mixture with your hands and press it into a round with raised edges, about 16 cm/6¼ in in diameter and 5 mm/¼ in thick on the lined baking sheet. Repeat with the remaining cauli mixture to make four pizza bases in total. Bake for 20 minutes, swapping the trays round halfway, until firm and golden.

4. While the bases are cooking, make the tomato sauce. Blend everything together with the remaining oregano until smooth. Spoon the sauce on top of the cooked pizza bases. Sprinkle over your choice of toppings, then the mozzarella cheese, then drizzle over a little olive oil. Bake for 10 minutes until the mozzarella melts. Serve topped with Parmesan shavings, if using, and basil leaves with a mixed salad on the side.

From 10 months

For babies

Sliced into wedges and topped with just cheese and tomato, pizzette make great finger food!

.27

Eye-spy eggs

Eggs peeking out from tomato-y sauce – yummy! These eggs are 'baked' on the hob, so they're really simple to make. Serve them with crusty bread – which is just right for dipping in the runny yolks and mopping up the tangy sauce.

What you need

1 tablespoon **olive oil**

4 **spring onions**, finely chopped

2 **garlic** cloves, finely chopped

1 teaspoon **ground cumin**

1 teaspoon mild **smoked paprika**

1 teaspoon **dried thyme**

400 g/14 oz can **chopped tomatoes**

4 **eggs**

2 tablespoons **coriander** leaves (optional)

Sprinkling of **dried chilli flakes** (optional)

Crusty wholemeal bread, to serve

What to do

1) Heat the oil in a frying pan with a tight-fitting lid over a medium heat. Add the spring onions and cook for 3 minutes until softened. Stir in the garlic, spices and thyme followed by the chopped tomatoes, then bring the sauce almost to the boil. Reduce the heat, part-cover with a lid and simmer for 5 minutes until the sauce has reduced and thickened.

2) Make 4 evenly spaced dips in the sauce using the back of a spoon. Crack an egg into each dip, cover the pan with a lid and cook gently for 10 minutes or until the egg whites are set but the yolks are still a little runny (see note for little ones).

3) Sprinkle the baked eggs with coriander, if using, and for adults a sprinkling of dried chilli flakes, if using, and serve with crusty bread on the side.

For babies

From 10 months

Make sure the eggs are cooked all the way through and then chop everything up to a perfect texture for your baby.

Zesty prawn pasta salad

serves 4 · prep 10 minutes · cook 10 minutes

This recipe is made using orzo, a pasta shaped like big grains of rice. Orzo is a good size for little ones who are ready to chew, and adds substance to a salad for everybody. The juicy prawns and veggies dressed with zesty yogurt sizzle with summer flavours.

What you need

225 g/8 oz **orzo pasta**

115 g/4 oz **frozen peas**

2 tablespoons **extra virgin olive oil**

200 g/7 oz **cooked prawns**

2 **courgettes**, coarsely grated or spiralized

2 **garlic** cloves, finely chopped

225 g/8 oz **cherry tomatoes**, chopped

Finely grated rind and juice of ½ small **lemon**

2 large handfuls of **rocket** leaves

Lemon yogurt dressing (optional)

Finely grated rind and juice of ½ small **lemon**

3 tablespoons **natural yogurt**

What to do

1. Cook the orzo according to the packet instructions (about 8–9 minutes), adding the peas 3 minutes before the end of the cooking time. Drain and leave to one side.

2. Meanwhile, to make the lemon yogurt, if using, mix together the half lemon rind and juice with the yogurt. Set aside.

3. Heat the oil in a large frying pan over a medium heat. Add the prawns, courgettes, garlic and tomatoes and cook for 30 seconds, stirring. Add the half lemon rind and juice, and the pasta and peas and stir until combined and warmed through.

4. Divide the rocket among four shallow bowls and top with the orzo mixture. Drizzle over the lemon yogurt before serving. You may prefer to serve the orzo without the lemon yogurt to young children.

Get grating!

Can I help?

Ask any willing sous-chef to help you grate the courgettes. Just make sure you watch those little fingers!

Family feasts

Wiggly chicken, cucumber + sugar snap noodles

serves **4** prep **15** minutes cook **5** minutes

Why is eating noodles so much fun? Twiddle them, slurp them, scoop them – everyone has their own favourite technique. With cucumber and sugar snap peas mixed in, this noodle dish is not only slurpy, it gives good crunch, too!

What you need

185 g/6½ oz **wholewheat noodles**

1 tablespoon **sunflower oil**

2 large **spring onions**, sliced diagonally, white and green parts separated

175 g/6 oz **cooked chicken**, shredded

85 g/3 oz **sugar snap peas**, sliced diagonally

6-cm/2½-in piece of **cucumber**, quartered lengthways, deseeded, and cut into chunks

2 **garlic** cloves, finely chopped

2.5-cm/1-in piece of fresh **root ginger**, peeled and finely chopped (optional)

2 **eggs**, lightly beaten

1 tablespoon reduced-salt **soy sauce**

A splash of **sesame oil**

Sweet chilli sauce (optional)

What to do

1. Cook the noodles in a saucepan of boiling water, following the packet instructions (about 5 minutes), until tender.

2. Meanwhile, heat a large wok over a high heat. Add the oil, the white spring onions, the chicken, sugar snap peas, cucumber, garlic and ginger, if using, and stir-fry for 2 minutes until the chicken is heated through and the vegetables just tender.

3. Make a well in the centre, pour in the eggs and stir until the eggs start to cook and scramble (about 3 minutes), then mix them into the rest of the ingredients in the wok.

4. Drain the noodles, reserving 3 tablespoons of the cooking water and add them both to the wok with the soy sauce and sesame oil. Turn briefly until everything is combined and then serve in bowls, sprinkled with the green part of the spring onions and with sweet chilli sauce for the grown-ups, if using.

For babies

From 10 months

Soy sauce is a bit too salty for little ones, so leave it out. Then, chop up the dish to your baby's usual texture.

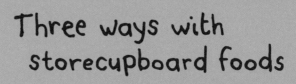

Three ways with storecupboard foods

It's the day before your big food shop and you need to be inventive… These suppers, using mostly staples from the food cupboards or the freezer, can help you to create delicious emergency family dinners.

Crispy crumb spaghetti with tuna

serves 4 | prep 5 minutes | cook 15 minutes | freeze me

300 g/10½ oz **spaghetti**

200 g/7 oz **frozen broccoli florets**

2 tablespoons **extra virgin olive oil**

50 g/1¾ oz **wholemeal breadcrumbs**, or made fresh using day-old bread

1 **garlic** clove, finely chopped

Finely grated zest and juice of 1 **lemon**

225 g/8 oz can **tuna chunks** in spring water, drained

1 tablespoon **capers**, patted dry (optional)

Cook the spaghetti in a saucepan of boiling water, following the instructions on the packet (about 10–15 minutes). Meanwhile, steam the broccoli for 2–3 minutes until just tender, then refresh under cold running water.

While the spaghetti and broccoli are cooking, heat 1 tablespoon of oil in a large frying pan. Add the breadcrumbs and fry for 4 minutes, then add the garlic and stir for 1 minute until the crumbs are crisp and light golden. Tip them into a bowl and stir in the lemon zest.

Wipe the frying pan clean, add the remaining oil, then the tuna, broccoli and capers, if using, and heat through. Drain the pasta, reserving the liquid, and add 100 ml/3½ fl oz of the cooking water with the lemon juice to the pan and heat through.

To serve, top the tuna spaghetti with the crumb mixture. (You could turn any leftover pasta and sauce into a tortilla: simply pour beaten eggs over the pasta mixture and cook both sides until set.)

Nutty coconut chicken

serves 4 · prep 15 minutes · cook 10 minutes · freeze me · 10+

175 g/6 oz **wholewheat noodles**

1 tablespoon **sunflower oil**

400 g/14 oz defrosted **frozen chicken breast strips**

100 g/3½ oz **frozen sliced mixed peppers**

3 **spring onions**, green and white parts separated, sliced

85 g/3 oz **frozen peas** or **frozen sliced green beans**

2 **garlic** cloves, finely chopped

2 teaspoons **garam masala**

1 teaspoon **turmeric**

2 tablespoons **smooth peanut butter**

½ can **coconut milk**

Cook the noodles in a saucepan of boiling water, following the packet instructions, until tender. Drain, refresh under cold running water, then leave to drain.

Meanwhile, heat the oil in a large wok over a high heat. Add the chicken and stir-fry for 4 minutes, or until cooked through. Remove from the wok with a slotted spoon and add the mixed peppers, the white part of the spring onions, the peas or beans and a splash more oil, if needed. Stir-fry for 2 minutes, then add the garlic and spices.

Reduce the heat to medium and add 125 ml/4 fl oz of water, the peanut butter and coconut milk. Stir until combined, then return the chicken to the pan with the noodles and warm through. Serve sprinkled with the green part of the spring onions.

Summer bean + carrot pot

serves 4–6 · prep 10 minutes · cook 30 minutes · freeze me · 10+

2 tablespoons **olive oil**

1 large **onion**, chopped

½ can **chopped tomatoes**

375 ml/13 fl oz reduced-salt **vegetable stock**

2 teaspoons **dried oregano**

1 can **cannellini beans**, drained

75 g/2½ oz stale **wholemeal bread**, torn into chunks

250 g/9 oz **frozen sliced carrots**

175 g/6 oz **frozen peas**

Wide strips of **lemon** zest and 1 tablespoon lemon juice

Bulgar wheat, to serve

Heat the oil in a flameproof casserole over a medium heat. Add the onion and cook for 5 minutes until softened. Add the tomatoes, stock, oregano and cannellini beans and bring to the boil, then reduce the heat to low, cover with a lid and simmer for 20 minutes, or until the beans are tender. Stir the stew occasionally to prevent it sticking to the bottom of the pan.

Add the bread, carrots, peas and lemon zest and juice to the casserole and cook for 3–5 minutes, stirring occasionally, until the carrots and peas are tender. Remove the zest and serve with bulgar wheat on the side. (It's also delicious topped with a spoonful of hummus, if you have any.)

Warm + scrummy meatballs in gravy

Most families have a tried-and-tested meatball recipe – this is the Ella's Kitchen family favourite. Served with creamy gravy, mashed potatoes and cranberry jelly, these meatballs are warming through and through.

What you need

400 g/14 oz **pork mince**

1 small **onion**, grated

85 g/3 oz **fresh breadcrumbs** (made using day-old bread)

4 tablespoons chopped **dill** (optional)

2 teaspoons **Dijon mustard**

1 **egg**, lightly beaten

2 tablespoons **sunflower oil**

Freshly ground **black pepper**

Mashed potatoes, seasonal vegetables, and **cranberry jelly** (optional), to serve

For the creamy gravy

30 g/1 oz **unsalted butter**

2 tablespoons **plain flour**

500 ml/17 fl oz reduced-salt **beef stock**

2 tablespoons **crème fraîche**

What to do

1. To make the meatballs, mix together the mince, onion, breadcrumbs, half the dill, if using, mustard and egg in a large bowl until combined. Season with pepper. With wet hands, roll the mixture into about 28 meatballs each a little bigger than the size of a large marble.

2. Heat the oil in a large frying pan over a medium–high heat. Add half the meatballs and cook for 5 minutes until browned all over. Remove with a slotted spoon, then cook the remaining meatballs, adding a splash more oil, if needed. Set aside on a plate while you make the sauce.

3. Melt the butter in the same frying pan over a medium–low heat. Stir in the flour and cook for 2 minutes, stirring continuously. Gradually pour in the stock and cook for 5 minutes, stirring continuously, until reduced and thickened. Stir in the crème fraîche, season with pepper, and return the meatballs to the pan. Stir in the remaining dill, if using, and cook until the meatballs have heated through (about 3 minutes). Serve the meatballs and gravy with mashed potatoes and seasonal vegetables, and with a spoonful of cranberry jelly, if using.

Pop-it-in-the-oven risotto with pesto

serves **4** (with extra pesto) · prep **15** minutes · cook **35** minutes · freeze me **10+** (risotto only)

There are so many reasons to love this brightly coloured risotto. Baking it in the oven means no more standing at the hob stirring away, and the broccoli pesto adds a special topping that crams in the vitamins for the whole family.

What you need

1 tablespoon **olive oil**

15 g/½ oz **unsalted butter**

1 large **onion**, finely chopped

85 g/3 oz **white cabbage**, finely chopped

1 teaspoon **dried oregano**

2 large **garlic** cloves, finely chopped

280 g/10 oz **risotto rice**

400 g/14 oz can **chopped tomatoes**

700 ml/1¼ pints reduced-salt **vegetable stock**

1 tablespoon **tomato purée**

For the broccoli pesto

40 g/1½ oz **cashew nuts**

4 **broccoli** florets (about 70 g/2½ oz)

15 g/½ oz **kale**, tough stalks removed

1 **garlic** clove, peeled

125 ml/4 fl oz **olive oil**

40 g/1½ oz **pecorino or Parmesan cheese**, finely grated, plus extra to serve (optional)

What to do

1. Preheat the oven to 180°C/350°F/Gas Mark 4. Heat the oil and butter in a flameproof casserole over a medium heat. Add the onion and cabbage and cook for 5 minutes, stirring occasionally, until softened.

2. Add the oregano, garlic and rice and cook for about 2 minutes, stirring. Pour in the tomatoes and stock and stir in the tomato purée and bring up to the boil. Stir well until combined, cover with a lid and place in the oven for 25 minutes, stirring halfway, or until the rice is cooked. Remove the risotto from the oven and leave to stand for 5 minutes.

3. Meanwhile, make the broccoli pesto. Put the cashews in a large, dry frying pan and toast over a medium–low heat for 4 minutes, turning once, until golden. Tip into a food processor and blitz until finely chopped. Add the broccoli, kale and garlic and process again until you have a coarse paste (you may have to occasionally scrape the mixture down the sides of the processor so it is evenly mixed).

4. With the motor still running, gradually pour in the oil until blended. Finally, stir in the pecorino or Parmesan. Serve the risotto topped with a good spoonful of the pesto and grate over extra cheese, if you like.

Tasty
treats
and
puds

Just-for-one mini cheesecakes

These cheesecakes may be little in size, but they're big on the flavour of tangy lemon and fragrant peaches. Made in a muffin tin, each cheesecake is a perfect size just for one.

What you need

For the base

40 g/1½ oz **unsalted butter**, plus extra for greasing

80 g/3 oz **pecan nuts**

50 g/1¾ oz **porridge oats**

30 g/1 oz **ground almonds**

1 tablespoon **maple syrup** or **clear honey**

For the filling

175 g/6 oz **cream cheese**

100 g/3½ oz **natural yogurt**

Finely grated rind of 1 **lemon** and juice of ½ lemon

2 tablespoons **maple syrup** or **clear honey**

1 teaspoon **vanilla extract**

1 large **egg**, lightly beaten

1½ teaspoons **cornflour**

4 ripe **peaches**, halved, stoned and chopped

What to do

1. Preheat the oven to 180°C/350°F/Gas Mark 4. Grease and line 10 holes of a muffin tin with baking parchment by cutting 2 folded strips of baking parchment and pressing them into the first hole to form a cross shape. Repeat with the remaining holes.

2. To make the cheesecake base, whiz the pecans and oats in a mini food processor, then tip them into a bowl and stir in the ground almonds. Melt the butter in a small saucepan with the maple syrup or honey, then stir it into the pecan mixture. Divide the mixture evenly among the prepared muffin tin holes and press it down to make a firm base. Bake for 5 minutes, then remove from the oven.

3. To make the filling, beat together all the ingredients, apart from the peaches, until smooth and creamy. Spoon the mixture over the nutty base and level the tops, then return to the oven for a further 15–20 minutes until firm and just set – the filling should still have a slight wobble. Leave to cool in the tin, then chill for 20 minutes.

4. When ready to serve, remove the cheesecakes from the muffin tin and peel off the paper strips. Spoon the peaches on top before serving.

From 10 months

For babies

Make the cheesecakes with maple syrup instead of honey to serve to babies. A mashed-up half portion will be enough.

Sticky sesame bananas

serves 4 | prep 5 minutes | cook 10 minutes

Take a banana, make it sticky, then sprinkle over some seeds – it's food that's fun to help with and delicious to eat. Who can stretch highest as they sprinkle?

What you need

2 teaspoons **sesame seeds**

30 g/1 oz **coconut oil** or **unsalted butter**

4 small **bananas**, peeled and halved lengthways

1 tablespoon **maple syrup** or **clear honey**

4 tablespoons **coconut drinking milk**

Thick natural yogurt, to serve

What to do

(1) Put the sesame seeds in a large, dry frying pan over a medium–low heat and toast for 3 minutes, stirring occasionally, or until they start to turn golden. Tip into a bowl and leave to one side.

(2) Melt the coconut oil or butter in the frying pan over a medium heat. Add the bananas and cook for 3 minutes until golden, turning once, and spooning the oil over the bananas as they cook.

(3) Place the bananas on serving plates. Add the maple syrup or honey and the coconut drinking milk to the pan, stir and cook briefly over a low heat until caramelized. Spoon the sauce over the bananas, sprinkle with sesame seeds and serve with yogurt.

Four ways with fruit

Encouraging little ones to eat a variety of fruits is one important way to make sure they get all the goodness they need for tip-top growing. Seeing grown-ups eat fruit, too, means setting the best example. Here are four simple ways to make delicious fruit treats for everyone to enjoy at family mealtimes.

Mango + passion fruit trifles

serves 4 · prep 10 minutes · freeze me

4 slices of **brioche**, torn into pieces

1 **mango**, halved, stoned and flesh scooped out

Juice of 3 **clementines** and finely grated rind of ½ clementine

150 ml/5 fl oz **thick natural yogurt**

175 ml/6 fl oz **homemade custard** (see page 137), or **ready-made fresh custard**

2 **passion fruits**, halved

Arrange the brioche in 4 tumblers or sundae glasses. Blend the mango with the clementine juice, then stir in the rind. Spoon the mixture on top of the brioche.

Mix together the yogurt and custard and spoon on top of the mango mixture, then chill until ready to serve.

When ready, scoop out the seeds and flesh from the passion fruit and pile them on top of the trifles.

Poached vanilla + black pepper strawberries

serves 4 · prep 5 minutes · cook 10 minutes

400 ml/14 fl oz fresh **orange juice**

2 teaspoons **clear honey** or **maple syrup**

1 teaspoon **vanilla extract**

300 g/10½ oz **strawberries**, hulled, halved if large

Freshly ground **black pepper**

Cream, **yogurt** or **ice cream**, to serve

Put the orange juice, honey or maple syrup and vanilla in a pan over a medium heat and bring almost to the boil. Reduce the heat to low and simmer for 5–7 minutes until syrupy.

Add the strawberries and a grinding of black pepper and turn until the strawberries are coated in the syrup, then spoon them into a bowl and leave to cool. The poached strawberries will keep in the fridge, covered, for up to 3 days.

Spiced cherry, berry + apple stew

serves 4 · prep 5 minutes · cook 10 minutes · freeze me · 10+

350 g/12 oz **frozen stoned cherries**

100 g/3½ oz **frozen blueberries**

1 **apple**, peeled, cored and diced

3 tablespoons **apple juice**

5 **cloves**

½ **cinnamon stick**

Natural yogurt, to serve

Put all the ingredients except the yogurt in a small saucepan over a medium–high heat and bring almost to the boil, then reduce the heat to low and simmer for 10 minutes until the fruit has softened.

Leave the fruit to cool slightly, then remove the cloves and cinnamon stick. Serve warm or cold with natural yogurt.

Dippy fruit fondue

serves 4 · prep 10 minutes · freeze me

½ large **cantaloupe melon**, cut in half around its middle

About 200 g/7 oz **favourite fruit**, such as strawberries, peaches, grapes, raspberries, kiwi fruit, blueberries or nectarines

5 tablespoons fresh **orange juice**

For the fruity dipping sauce

250 g/9 oz **raspberries**

A good squeeze of **lime**

A drizzle of **clear honey** or **maple syrup**, to taste

Using a spoon, scoop the seeds out of the centre of the melon half. Slice a sliver off the base of the melon so that it stands up and place the melon on a serving plate. Scoop out most of the flesh with a melon baller to make a bowl shape with a 1-cm/½-in border.

Prepare your fruit (peeling, chopping, slicing and deseeding as necessary). Mix the fruit, including the melon balls, with the orange juice, then spoon it into the melon bowl, pouring over any juice.

To make the fruity dipping sauce, blend the raspberries with the lime juice. Taste and sweeten with honey or maple syrup as needed. To serve, either use cocktail sticks, little forks, or fingers to dunk the fruit from the melon bowl into the dipping sauce.

Strawberry clouds

Oh-so floaty, these light, sweet omelettes are like delicious clouds on your plate. Just be careful they don't float away before you eat them all up!

What you need

300 g/10 oz **strawberries**, hulled and halved

3 **eggs**, separated and set aside individually

2 teaspoons **clear honey**

1 teaspoon **vanilla extract**

2 teaspoons **coconut or sunflower oil**

Thick cream or **natural yogurt** and 2 handfuls of **blueberries**, halved, to serve

What to do

1. Mash or purée half the strawberries to make a fruit sauce, then set aside. Using a hand whisk, whisk the egg whites in a grease-free bowl until they form soft peaks. Gradually add the honey and vanilla, whisking until the whites are stiff and glossy. Fold in the yolks.

2. Preheat the grill to medium–high. Melt half the oil in a large frying pan with a heatproof handle and swirl to coat the base. Tip a large serving spoonful of the frothy egg mixture into the pan and spread it out with a spatula into a round. Repeat with a second serving spoonful to cook two 'clouds' at once. Cook over a medium–low heat for 2–3 minutes until the base is set and light golden. Transfer the pan to the grill and cook the top until just set.

3. Slide the 'clouds' onto a serving plate and top with mashed or puréed strawberries, the cream or yogurt and the halved strawberries and blueberries. Repeat, making clouds two at a time, until all the mixture is used up.

Ella's shortcut

Instead of making a strawberry sauce, use 1 x 120 g pouch of Ella's Kitchen strawberries + apples.

Time for a family get-together!

Where's mine?

Whether you're cooking Sunday lunch for granny and grandpa or a special birthday celebration with all your family and friends, you'll find this chapter packed with tummy-filling crowd-pleasers.

Lazy-day lamb with tahini yogurt

serves 6–8 | prep 20 minutes | cook 4 hours | freeze me 10+
+ marinating

This tasty family feast is slow cooked, so it leaves you lots of time to join in with the party. It's a sociable dish – everyone piles in and wraps up their favourite food!

What you need

1.3 kg/3 lb **lamb shoulder** on the bone

2 **carrots**, peeled and quartered lengthways

1 **onion**, cut into wedges

1 long **rosemary** sprig

Pomegranate seeds, **mint** leaves, **flatbreads**, **lemon** wedges, and shredded **carrot** and **salad leaves**, to serve

For the marinade

1 tablespoon **mixed spice**

4 teaspoons **ground cumin**

3 **garlic** cloves, crushed

1 tablespoon **olive oil**

Finely grated rind and juice of 1 **lemon**

1 tablespoon **clear honey**

Freshly ground **black pepper**

For the tahini yogurt sauce (optional)

150 ml/5 fl oz **Greek yogurt**

2 tablespoons **tahini**

1 **garlic** clove, crushed

2 tablespoons **lemon** juice

What to do

1. Pat the lamb dry and make several slashes across the top. Mix together all the marinade ingredients and rub the mixture all over the lamb, making sure it gets into the cuts. Put the carrots, onion and rosemary in a roasting tin, top with the lamb, cover and marinate at room temperature for 1 hour.

2. Preheat the oven to its highest setting.

3. Add a good splash of water to the lamb tin, cover with a double layer of foil and put it in the oven. Immediately turn the oven temperature down to 160°C/315°F/Gas Mark 2–3 and roast for 3 hours.

4. Remove the foil, baste the lamb with any juices in the base of the tin and roast, uncovered, for another 1 hour until the lamb is very tender. Remove from the oven, cover with foil and a clean tea towel and leave to rest for 15 minutes.

5. Meanwhile, mix together all the ingredients for the tahini yogurt sauce and warm the flatbreads in the oven. Serve the lamb pulled into chunks, or shredded with forks, rather than carved. Skim off and discard any fat in the base of the roasting tin, then spoon some of the pan juices over the shredded lamb.

6. Place the lamb on a wooden board, scatter over the pomegranate seeds and mint leaves and serve with flatbreads, lemon wedges, tahini yogurt sauce and salad on the side.

Crispy topped pork stroganoff

A melt-in-your-mouth kind of dinner, this stroganoff is so good you'll be creating family gatherings just so you have a reason to make this big, wholesome dish. The rösti topping makes a brilliant alternative to mash, and gives the stroganoff a good crunch.

What you need

2 tablespoons **olive oil**

1 **onion**, chopped

2 **leeks**, chopped

250 g/9 oz **button mushrooms**, halved if large

500 g/1 lb 2 oz **pork shoulder or leg**, diced

1 heaped tablespoon **plain flour**

2 large **garlic** cloves, chopped

1 tablespoon chopped **rosemary**

2 **bay leaves**

2 teaspoons **mild smoked paprika**

300 ml/½ pint reduced-salt **chicken stock**

3 tablespoons **soured cream**

450 g/1 lb **new potatoes**, such as Charlotte

40 g/1½ oz **unsalted butter**, diced

Speed it up!

Use pork fillet instead of shoulder or leg and serve just the stroganoff mixture with rice or mash on the side, instead of baking with the rosti. All the deliciousness in less time!

What to do

1. Heat half the oil in a large saucepan over a medium heat. Add the onion, leeks and mushrooms and cook for 5 minutes, stirring, until softened. Remove from the pan with a slotted spoon and set aside.

2. Dust the pork in the flour. Pour the rest of the oil into the pan over a medium–high heat, add the pork and cook for 5 minutes, stirring, until browned all over. Return the vegetables to the pan with the garlic, herbs and paprika, then pour in the stock and stir until combined. Bring to the boil, then reduce the heat, part-cover with a lid and simmer for 15 minutes until the sauce has reduced and thickened. Remove the bay leaves, stir in the soured cream and warm through.

3. Meanwhile, preheat the oven to 200°C/400°F/ Gas Mark 6. Cook the potatoes in a large saucepan of boiling water for 10–15 minutes until tender. Drain, then when cool enough to handle, peel off the skins and coarsely grate into a bowl. Gently stir in half the butter.

4. Spoon the pork mixture into a shallow, ovenproof dish, then spoon the potato mixture on top in an even layer. Dot the top with the remaining butter and cook in the oven for 25 minutes or until the top starts to turn golden.

 Food outdoors is such fun, especially when there are lots of you to eat and play. We can't promise sunshine, but we can promise some yummy ideas for picnics and barbecues with family and friends!

Laid-back crustless quiche

serves 8–12 · prep 10 minutes · cook 40 minutes · freeze me 10+

With potatoes on the inside, this quiche is filling even without a pastry casing! Take it on a family picnic, or put it in packed lunch for nursery, school or work.

What you need

350 g/12 oz **new potatoes**, halved if large

Unsalted butter, for greasing

8 **eggs**, lightly beaten

7 **spring onions**, sliced

100 g/3½ oz **sun-dried tomatoes** in oil, drained and chopped

A handful of **basil** leaves

1 tablespoon **oregano** or **thyme** leaves

175 ml/6 fl oz **whole milk**

140 g/5 oz **Gruyère cheese**, grated

Freshly ground **black pepper**

What to do

1. Boil the potatoes for 10–15 minutes until tender. Drain and cool slightly, then remove the skins and cut into bite-sized chunks.

2. Grease and line a 23-cm/9-in square cake tin. Preheat the oven to 180°C/350°F/Gas Mark 4.

3. Beat the eggs in a large bowl and add the rest of the ingredients, including the cooked potatoes. Season, and stir to combine. Pour the mixture into the prepared tin and bake for 35–40 minutes until set. Cool for 5 minutes, then turn out of the tin and cut into squares.

Find it!

Just for fun

A family picnic is the perfect opportunity for a scavenger hunt that tunes in to the sights, sounds and scents of the great outdoors. Make a list of items for everyone to find – try to think of one or two for each sense. Here are some ideas:

🙂 Touch: a smooth stone + a rough leaf

🙂 Smell: a flower + tree bark

🙂 Sight: something yellow + something speckled

🙂 Sound: a crunchy leaf + a snapping stick

🙂 Taste: a blackberry (ensure an adult checks this before anything goes into little mouths)

Five ways to dip + dunk

Kids love dipping and dunking. These dips make excellent picnic or lunchbox fillers. Serve them with breadsticks or veggie batons, or spread them on toast, which you then cut into crustless fingers for babies over 7 months.

Roasted carrot dip

serves 6–8 | prep 10 minutes | cook 50 minutes | freeze me 7+

1 **sweet potato** (about 250 g/9 oz total weight)

3 large **carrots**, peeled and quartered lengthways

3 tablespoons **extra virgin olive oil**

1 **garlic** clove, crushed

2 tablespoons **tahini**

½–1 teaspoon **ras el hanout** or **harissa** (optional)

Juice of 1 **lemon**

Preheat the oven to 200°C/400°F/Gas Mark 6. Bake the sweet potato in the oven for 50 minutes, or until tender.

Meanwhile, toss the carrots in 1 tablespoon of the oil to coat, tip them onto a baking sheet in an even layer and roast (in the same oven as the potato) for 35–40 minutes, until tender and starting to colour. Peel the sweet potato and put the flesh in a food processor with the roasted carrots and the rest of the ingredients and blend until smooth and creamy.

Tunasalata

serves 6–8 | prep 10 minutes | cook 10 minutes | 10+

175 g/6 oz **potato**, peeled and cut into small chunks, or **stale crustless bread**

Juice of 1 **lemon** and finely grated rind of ½ lemon

½ small **onion**, finely grated

1 tablespoon **mayonnaise**

200 g/7 oz can **tuna chunks** in olive oil, drained, reserving the oil (supplement with **extra virgin olive oil**, if insufficient oil in the can)

Freshly ground **black pepper**

If using potato, cook the cubes in a pan of boiling water for 10 minutes or until tender, then drain and tip into a large bowl. Add 3 tablespoons of the oil from the fish and the lemon juice and mash until smooth. Add the onion, lemon rind, mayonnaise and tuna to the potato mixture and mash with a fork until combined, then season with pepper to taste.

If using bread, soak it briefly in cold water until soft, then drain and squeeze out any excess water. Place in a blender with the rest of the ingredients and blend until smooth, then season with pepper to taste.

Apple raita

1 **red eating apple** (skin on), cored and coarsely grated

3 heaped tablespoons chopped **mint**

Juice of ½ **lime**

125 ml/4 fl oz **natural yogurt**

1 small **garlic** clove, crushed (optional)

Mix together all the ingredients for the raita in a bowl, adding the garlic, if using, and mixing again to combine.

Minty pea + ricotta dip

175 g/6 oz **frozen peas**

100 g/3½ oz **ricotta cheese**

2 **spring onions**, thinly sliced

Juice and finely grated rind of 1 **lemon**

6 heaped tablespoons roughly chopped **mint**

4 tablespoons **natural yogurt**

Cook the peas in a pan of boiling water until tender (about 5 minutes), then drain and tip them into a blender with the ricotta, spring onions, lemon juice, mint and yogurt. Blend everything together until smooth and creamy. Spoon the dip into a bowl and stir in the lemon rind.

Smoky aubergine dip

1 **aubergine**

1 tablespoon **olive oil**

1 small **garlic** clove, crushed

1 tablespoon **tahini**

3 tablespoons **natural yogurt**

½ teaspoon **mild smoked paprika**

Juice of ½ **lemon**

2 tablespoons finely chopped **flat-leaf parsley**

Preheat the oven to 200°C/400°F/Gas Mark 6. Prick the aubergine all over with a fork and then brush with a little of the oil. Place the aubergine on a baking sheet and roast for 45 minutes, or until the flesh is nice and soft. Cut the aubergine in half, scoop out the flesh, discarding any particularly seedy bits. Mash or blend the aubergine with the remaining oil, and the garlic, tahini, yogurt, paprika and lemon juice. Stir in the parsley and spoon into a bowl.

Sprinkled Brazilian pineapple sticks

Put on your carnival hat and have a festival with these griddled pineapple chunks.
Who in the family can dance the best samba?

What you need

1 small **pineapple**

Clear honey, for brushing

A handful of **goji berries**, for sprinkling (optional)

Coconut yogurt or **thick natural yogurt**, to serve

For the coconut sprinkle

4 tablespoons **unsweetened desiccated coconut**

1 tablespoon **sesame seeds**

40 g/1½ oz **cashew nuts**

½ teaspoon **ground cinnamon**

What to do

1. Soak 4 wooden skewers in cold water for 30 minutes (or use metal skewers). Heat the barbecue or preheat the grill to high. Remove the leafy top of the pineapple and then stand the pineapple upright on a chopping board. Slice off the skin, then cut the pineapple into quarters lengthways. Remove the hard core, then cut each quarter into 1-cm/½-in thick slices.

2. Thread the pineapple onto the prepared skewers – about 8 pieces on each skewer. Barbecue or grill the pineapple for 5 minutes. Lightly brush with honey and cook for another 5 minutes, turning occasionally.

3. Meanwhile, make the coconut sprinkle. Toast the coconut in a dry frying pan for 2 minutes, or until it starts to colour, tossing occasionally. Tip into a bowl. Toast the sesame seeds in the same pan for 3 minutes, or until starting to colour. Add them to the coconut. Toast the cashews for 4 minutes, turning once, or until slightly golden. Finely chop the cashews and add to the bowl with the cinnamon, then stir to combine.

4. Sprinkle the pineapple with coconut sprinkle and with goji berries, if using, and serve with yogurt on the side. Alternatively, spoon some yogurt into a bowl, and top with pineapple chunks, goji berries, if using, and sprinkle.

The .... Family's Meal Planner

write your name here →

This week's foody adventures

Our family shopping list

1 ....
2 ....
3 ....
4 ....
5 ....
6 ....
7 ....
8 ....
9 ....
10 ....
11 ....
12 ....
13 ....
14 ....
15 ....

	Breakfast	Lunch	Dinner	This week's special guests	Who needs a lunchbox?
Monday					
Tuesday					
Wednesday					
Thursday					
Friday					
Saturday					
Sunday					

Cooking together!

Let's cook together on ....

Let's make ....

....
....
....

STEP INTO THE WORLD OF

ANCIENT

EGYPT

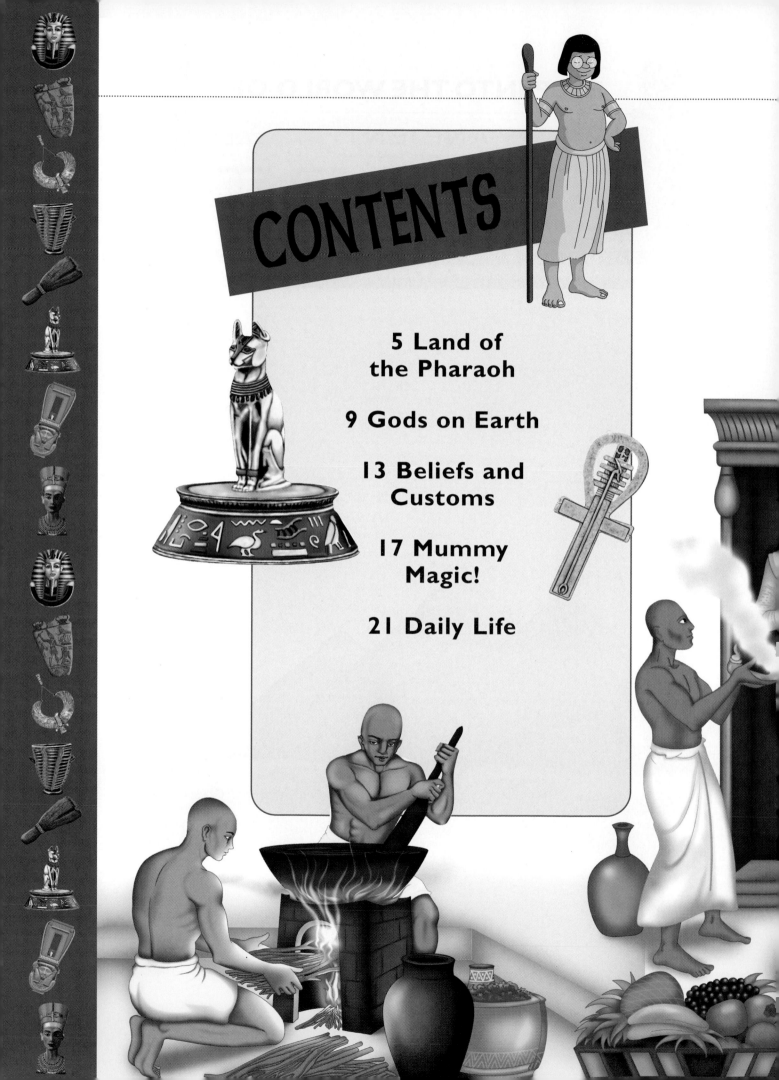

CONTENTS

CONTENTS

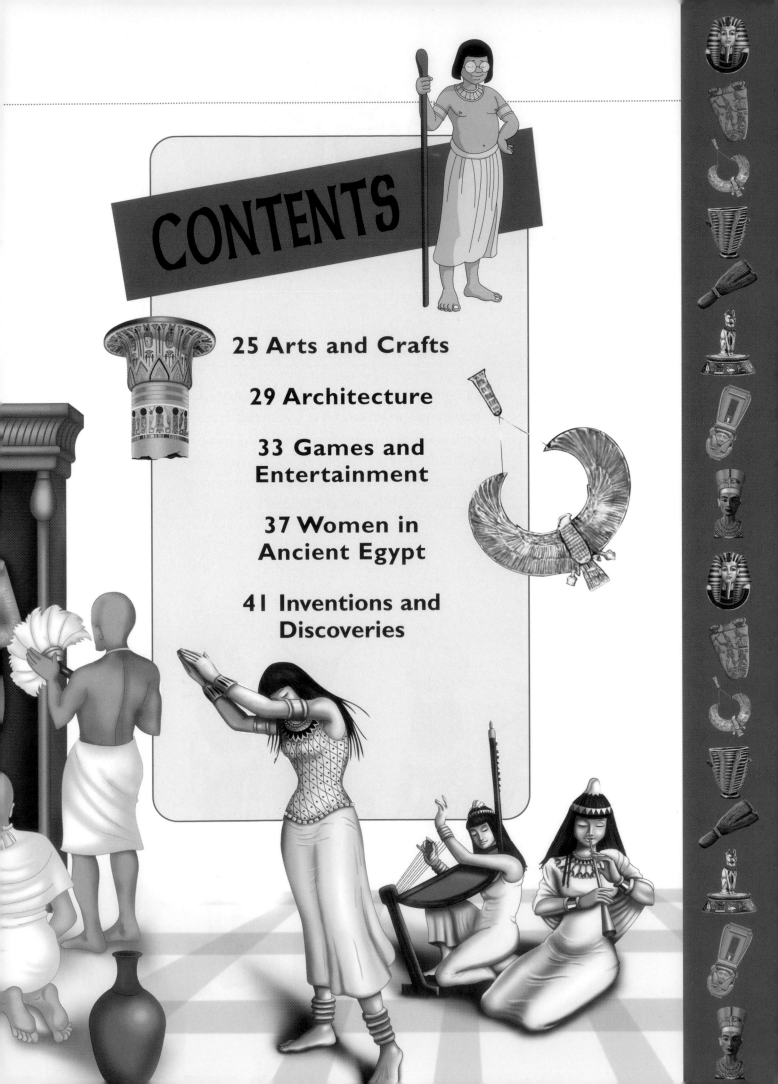

LAND OF THE PHARAOH

Ancient Egypt is one of the world's longest-lasting civilisations. Its rulers (pharaohs) turned it into one of the most powerful empires there ever was.

Remarkable Rulers

Queen Hatshepsut was the first female pharaoh of Egypt, while Cleopatra VII was the last. Another legendary ruler was Ramses II, under whose reign the Egyptian empire reached its peak.

Perhaps the most famed pharaoh of all time was Tutankhamun. At the age of nine, he became the youngest pharaoh, and was also called the "boy king". Although Tutankhamun was not an important ruler, he became famous when his tomb was uncovered and it was revealed as the only Egyptian royal tomb to have not been robbed!

Pharaoh Power

Pharaohs were believed to have been sent to earth by the gods in heaven. They were worshipped like gods, and were seen as the spiritual link between the gods and the common people.

Pharaohs lived in palaces and possessed enormous wealth. During their travels, they would sit in carrying chairs. Cushioned seats were attached to poles so that the chair could be lifted on men's shoulders.

Pharaohs and other important people travelled from one place to another on luxurious carrying chairs

LAND OF THE PHARAOH

 ### When was the ancient Egyptian civilisation born?

The civilisation of ancient Egypt began around 5,000 years ago, with the reign of King Menes. He united Upper and Lower Egypt into one kingdom. This is believed to have begun the first Egyptian dynasty, or family of rulers, in 3100 B.C.

The Nemes headdress was a royal, blue-and-gold striped headpiece made of stiff cloth

Pharaohs wore colourful linen clothes that were decorated with beads and golden threads

 ### How many dynasties ruled ancient Egypt?

About 30 dynasties ruled during the different periods of the ancient Egyptian civilisation. These periods – roughly extending from about 3100 B.C. to A.D. 395 – were the Late Predynastic Period, the Early Dynastic Period, the Old Kingdom, the First Intermediate Period, the Middle Kingdom, the Second Intermediate Period, the New Kingdom, the Third Intermediate Period, the Late Period and the Greco-Roman Period.

What kind of clothes did Egyptian pharaohs wear?

Male pharaohs wore kilts made of fine linen and decorated with colourful sashes and ornaments. They wore leather sandals and carried staffs known as flails, which symbolised their power. Pharaohs also wore eye make-up and fake beards. Female pharaohs wore flowing tunics of fine cloth and lots of jewellery, make-up and decorative sandals.

What kind of powers were attributed to pharaohs in ancient Egypt?

The ancient Egyptians identified their pharaohs with various gods, including Horus, Ra and Osiris. The pharaoh was regarded as all-knowing and all-powerful, and endowed with supernatural powers. He had control over the whole country, and his word was supreme!

How many different types of crowns did pharaohs wear?

Pharaohs wore a variety of headdresses for different occasions. These included the Red Crown, the White Crown, the Khepresh (Blue) Crown, the Double Crown, the Atef Crown and the Nemes Headdress.

This White Crown belonged to King Osiris. Its sides were decorated by feathers

When did pharaohs wear the Khepresh Crown?

The Khepresh, or Blue, Crown, was worn by pharaohs during battles and ceremonies. These crowns were typically made of blue leather and richly decorated with ostrich feathers, gold or bronze sun disks, and figures of cobras.

The Khepresh Crown adorned the head of pharaohs during wars or ceremonies

What is the difference between the Red, White and Double crowns?

The White Crown represented a king's rule in Upper Egypt, while the Red Crown symbolised rule in Lower Egypt. The Double Crown, which combined both the White and Red crowns, symbolised a pharaoh's power over both Upper and Lower Egypt.

The Double Crown of the pharaoh was the ultimate symbol of power

LAND OF THE PHARAOH

Q **Which is the most well-known object found in King Tutankhamun's tomb?**

The most famous treasure uncovered from the royal tomb of Tutankhamun was his funerary mask. Made of gold and inlaid with precious stones, the mask was used to cover the face of the king's mummified body.

Q **When did the ancient Egyptian civilisation come to an end?**

The end of the ancient Egyptian civilisation started around 332 B.C., with the invasion of the Egyptian empire by Alexander the Great. About 30 B.C., the people of ancient Egypt became a part of the Roman Empire.

The famous mask of King Tut was made of pure gold, and covered the head and shoulders of the king's mummy

Q **Which pharaoh's wife was said to be the most beautiful woman to have ever lived in ancient Egypt?**

Queen Nefertiti, the royal wife of Pharaoh Akhenaten, was said to be the most beautiful woman in the history of ancient Egypt.

The bust of Queen Nefertiti is one of the most famous icons of ancient Egypt

Q **Did Egyptian pharaohs have pictures of their enemies on their shoes?**

Ancient Egyptian pharaohs wore wooden sandals with pictures of enemies on the soles. The treading of the pharaoh in these shoes symbolised the trampling of his enemies to defeat!

Q **Who was the only Egyptian queen to be mentioned in the Bible?**

Queen Tahpenes was the only Egyptian queen to find a place in the Bible. She ruled during the reigns of David and Solomon.

GODS ON EARTH

The Egyptian people worshipped many different deities as gods who lived on earth.

Animal Worship

The earliest Egyptians were known to practice animal worship. Some animals, like the cat, were considered very sacred. With time, the gods and goddesses were represented with animal heads and human bodies. This was because the Egyptians believed that their deities could appear in both human and animal forms. Goddess Bast (or Bastet), a very important deity, was represented in the form of half-woman, half-cat in sculptures. She symbolised joy, dancing and music, and health and healing.

This gold statue is of the Sacred Cat of Bast, which is associated with Goddess Bastet

Great Gods and Goddesses

The Egyptians grouped their deities in various ways. The most important grouping was the Great Ennead of Heliopolis, a council of the nine main deities of ancient Egypt – Ra (Atum), Shu, Tefnut, Geb, Nut, Osiris, Isis, Seth and Nephthys. The first five represented the five elements of nature: sun, air, moisture, earth and sky.

GODS ON EARTH

 What kind of deities did the ancient Egyptians worship?

Gods and goddesses in ancient Egypt often represented the forces of nature, such as the sun, sky, earth and wind. The people believed that their gods and goddesses lived on earth, and portrayed them with human bodies and animal heads.

 Why was the decoration of coffins so important?

The ancient Egyptians believed that if coffins were not decorated, the ka of a dead person would not be able to journey between the body and the afterlife!

Egyptian deities included Thoth (god of wisdom), Ra (sun god), Hathor (goddess of love), Khnum (creator god) and Anubis (god of the dead)

Scenes of Ramses II on his war chariot have often been depicted on the tomb walls of ancient Egypt

Who was regarded as the most important pharaoh of ancient Egypt?

Ramses II, also called Ramses the Great, was considered to be the most important pharaoh and god-king. Also known as "Horus", "Warrior King" and "Son of Ra", he ruled Egypt for about 66 years, during which he fought many important wars.

 How was the human body classified in ancient Egyptian religion?

According to ancient Egyptian religion, the human body was divided into 36 parts. A particular god or goddess was believed to protect each of these parts.

What were the ba and the ka?

The ba and the ka represented the spirits of the dead in ancient Egypt. It was commonly believed that everyone had a ba (soul) as well as a ka (an invisible twin). The ba and the ka were freed from the body after the person's death. The ba, which was depicted as a bird, could travel freely and kept in touch with friends and family members of the dead person. In the afterlife, the goal of the ba was to seek out the ka.

Who was the most important god in ancient Egypt?

The ancient Egyptians considered the sun god, Ra (or Re), as the creator of everything. He was represented with a man's body and a hawk's head. In his hand he held an ankh and a wand.

Which ancient Egyptian temples were moved from their original location?

In the 1960s, the temple complex in the island of Philae, in Aswan, Egypt, was moved to protect it from the rising water levels of the Nile River when the Aswan Dam was erected. The temples were put back together on the island of Agilkia.

The Philae Temple, located at the southernmost end of ancient Egypt, got its name from the Egyptian word pilak ("the end")

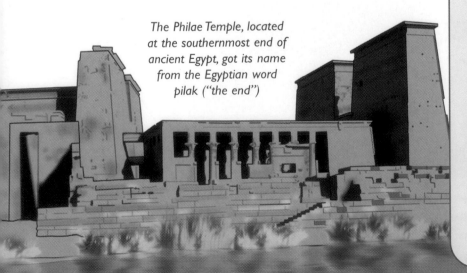

FACT BOX

■ Ancient Egyptian tablets suggest that the people used incense sticks during prayer. These sticks were probably placed in decorated holders or stands.

The religious Egyptians burned incense sticks on holders at temples and in their homes

■ Goddess Nut was the goddess of the sky in ancient Egypt. She was represented posing on her hands and feet, stretched in the shape of an arc across the sky. Her blue-coloured body was usually shown as covered in stars.

■ An ancient Egyptian legend relates that Seth, the wicked brother of Isis and Osiris, killed Osiris and scattered his body in 14 different parts. Isis gathered the pieces and magically bound them together with strips of cloth, and made the very first Egyptian mummy!

GODS ON EARTH

 In what state was the temple of Horus at Edfu discovered?

The temple at Edfu was almost entirely buried under the desert sands until the time it was discovered. Not surprisingly, it remains one of the best-preserved temples of ancient Egypt. It was built between 237 B.C. and 57 B.C. for Horus, the falcon-headed god.

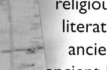

The Edfu Temple is regarded as the best-preserved temple of ancient Egypt

 Which ancient Egyptian statue represented the sun god?

In ancient Egypt, statues of the sphinx represented the sun god, with the facial features of the reigning pharaoh. The sphinx, a figure of a male lion with a human head, symbolised infinite wisdom.

 What leads up to the entrance of the Luxor Temple in Egypt?

The entrance to the Luxor Temple is lined with a row of over 60 sphinxes! The temple was built during the 18th dynasty to honour the god Amun.

What is the *Book of the Dead*?

The *Book of the Dead* is a collection of religious and magical literature written in ancient Egypt. The ancient Egyptians knew it as *The Chapter of Coming-Forth-by-Day*. Copies of this book, in the form of papyrus scrolls, were placed inside the tombs of important people.

What was the *menat*?

The *menat* was a beaded collar or necklace that was believed to have derived healing powers from the goddess Hathor.

The remains of an ancient church and and an Islamic mosque were discovered at the Luxor Temple

BELIEFS AND CUSTOMS

Ancient Egyptian rituals were based on people's faith in the gods, pharaohs, animal worship and the forces of nature.

Life and Death

Central to Egyptian religion was the belief in life after death. The soul moved on to a new world after leaving the body. It was thought that the god Osiris carried the body across the Nile into the afterlife.

Might of Magic

The Egyptians perceived the influence of magic in every aspect of life, from social customs to the practice of medicine. Their belief in an eternal life was depicted in several charms. The key-shaped ankh – resembling a T-shaped cross with a loop over it – represented health and happiness.

The ancient Egyptians had their share of unusual beliefs as well. One was that frogs and worms came from the deposits of the Nile River's floods! The black colour of the Nile's mineral-rich soil even led the people to believe that black was a lucky colour. Probably the strangest of their beliefs was that headaches and toothaches could be cured by eating fried mice!

The ankh, a symbol of eternal life in ancient Egypt, means "life" in the Egyptian language

BELIEFS AND CUSTOMS

How was religion related to the beliefs and customs of ancient Egypt?

Egyptian beliefs and customs revolved around religion. The people worshipped nearly 2,000 deites, in the form of idols at temples and shrines. It is said that people were only allowed up to the entrance of these temples, but could convey messages to the gods through priests, who were regarded as servants of the gods.

In ancient Egypt, a temple was the "house of god", and the god lived in idol form inside a shrine or a sanctuary

Why were scribes given a high social status in ancient Egypt

Scribes were the only ones in Egypt who could read and write, so they enjoyed a high status in society. They could perform many different tasks, like writing letters, keeping accounts and maintaining important records.

How was the social status of an ancient Egyptian decided?

A person's position in ancient Egyptian society was decided by the job he did. Thus, among the various classes were soldiers, farmers, craftsmen, engineers, priests and noblemen.

What kind of ancient Egyptian objects were thought to have magical qualities?

The people of ancient Egypt believed that amulets, or charms, had magical powers. Amulets were considered to bring good luck and health, and protect against evil forces.

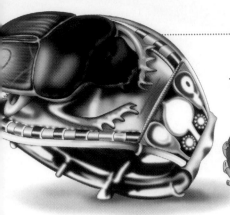

The Egyptians called the scarab beetle "Kheper"

 Which was the most popular Egyptian amulet?

The most common amulet in ancient Egypt was that of the scarab beetle. The scarab was the spiritual symbol of the god Ra. It represented eternal life.

What did the Egyptian custom of *inw* involve?

The *inw* was an important Egyptian custom of exchanging gifts between people of different social statuses.

What were the different social classes of ancient Egypt?

The social structure of ancient Egypt was like a pyramid. At the base was the majority of the population, comprising soldiers, farmers and tomb builders. Higher up were the skilled craftsmen, and above them were the scribes. Still higher were priests, doctors and engineers. Close to the top were high priests and noblemen, followed by the vizier, or the pharaoh's advisor. Finally, at the head was the pharaoh.

The pyramidal structure of society in ancient Egypt

FACT BOX

- According to an ancient Egyptian belief, shadows were one of the important elements that humans were made of. The shadow was thought to protect a person from harm.

- Special flasks were exchanged as gifts during New Year's Eve celebrations in ancient Egypt. These New Year flasks had inscriptions that were said to summon the gods, to bless the owners of the flasks with a healthy and happy life in the new year.

New Year flasks in ancient Egypt were filled with water from a sacred pool

- Egyptian marriages were not elaborate ceremonies. Two people were considered to be "married" when they moved into a common household together.

15

BELIEFS AND CUSTOMS

What is the Eye of Horus?

The Eye of Horus was the name of a common ancient Egyptian symbol. Also known as the "magic eye" or the *udjat*, it represented the eye of the god Horus. The eye featured commonly on amulets, and was believed to be a powerful symbol that protected people from evil and guided them along the right path.

Different parts of the Eye of Horus stood for fractions in mathematics, with the complete eye representing the value of "1"!

How did the ancient Egyptians cure illnesses?

According to the ancient Egyptians, illnesses were caused by angry gods or evil spirits that entered a person's body. Doctors and priests would use their knowledge and powers to get rid of illnesses. Their cures included amulets, magic spells and various potions.

What special association do wedding rings have with ancient Egypt?

The custom of wearing an engagement ring on the fourth finger of the left hand is said to have come from ancient Egypt. The Egyptians believed that the vein running from that particular finger was directly connected to the heart!

How did Egyptian pharaohs try to stop the effects of alcohol?

It is said that ancient Egyptian pharaohs ate lots of cabbage before they drank alcohol. They believed that this would allow them to drink without any side effects!

Did ancient Egyptians marry their siblings?

Ancient Egyptians were known to marry people they were related to. However, it was also common for unrelated couples to call each other "brother" or "sister" affectionately!

In ancient Egypt, the bride was usually 14-15 years old and the groom, around 17!

MUMMY MAGIC!

An interesting feature of the Egyptian civilisation was the elaborate rituals that followed from the people's faith in the afterlife.

Making Mummies

Ancient Egyptians took great care to preserve dead bodies, to aid the passage to the next world. They used a process called embalming, or mummification.

The body was first cleaned with salts, oils, wines and spices, and left to dry. Body parts were removed, dried and then stored separately in canopic jars. These jars were meant to call upon the protection of guardian gods, each for one specific organ. The jars were placed inside a canopic chest.

Finally, the body was wrapped in linen bandages, with amulets placed in between the layers, and placed in a coffin, which was buried inside a tomb.

Canopic jars had lids in the shape of human, baboon, falcon and jackal heads, symbolising the spirits of the four sons of Horus

Tomb Talk

The poor people were usually buried in ordinary, small coffins made of reed. Grand tombs were reserved for the royalty and other important people.

MUMMY MAGIC!

 What did the process of evisceration involve?

Before a dead body was wrapped up, all internal organs except the heart were removed. This process was known as evisceration.

 Which chemical was used for drying and preserving the body?

A salt deposit extracted from dried-up river beds was used to dry and cleanse dead bodies. It was known as natron.

 When did the ancient Egyptians begin to make mummies?

The ancient Egyptians started mummifying the bodies of royal and important people sometime in about 2400 B.C. The practice continued for nearly 3,000 years.

 What were linen strips, used for wrapping mummies, sometimes soaked in?

The linen strips used to wrap dead bodies were sometimes soaked in plaster to quicken the drying process.

Q Why did ancient Egyptians bury the bodies of dead people in pyramids?

Ancient Egyptians believed that preserving the body of a dead person would enable him to live comfortably in the afterlife. Therefore, they built elaborate pyramids to bury their dead.

The process of mummificatian lasted nearly two months!

Q How did the process of mummification come about?

The Egyptians thought of using mummification after they realised that the hot sands of the deserts and the surrounding climate dried up corpses, instead of turning them to dust.

Q Who were the people involved in mummification?

Mummification was a religious ceremony in ancient Egypt, and was performed by priests. One of the priests used to wear the jackal-shaped mask of Anubis, the god of the dead.

The funeral barges of ancient Egyptian pharaohs were also called "sun boats"

■ Before mummies were placed inside the tomb, a ceremony called the "Opening of the Mouth" was performed. The ritual was believed to "animate" the mummy so that it could eat, drink, breathe, see, hear and feel in the next world too!

■ Miniature statues called *shabti*s were placed in tombs to perform the role of servants to the mummy in the afterlife.

■ Initially, full-size boats were buried with mummies to transport them to the afterlife. However, it was a very expensive and time-consuming process. So, from the 12th Dynasty onwards, tiny models of boats began to be used.

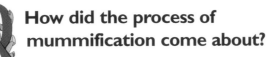

MUMMY MAGIC!

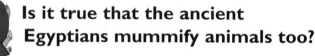

Q What kind of objects was buried along with the mummy?

Day-to-day objects and precious belongings were buried along with the mummy, so that he would have all he might need in the next life. Many treasures were found inside Tutankhamun's tomb, among them his gold scabbard and dagger, golden throne and jewellery chest.

Q Is it true that the ancient Egyptians mummify animals too?

Hundreds of mummified crocodiles, cats, snakes and other creatures have been found in Egypt. Some pets were buried alongside their mummified owners, while others were preserved because they were held sacred.

King Tut's dagger, made of gold, glass and precious stones, was found attached to the waist of his mummified body

The Egyptians used to mummify dogs as well, and placed them at the feet of their owners!

Q Why was the heart the only organ left inside the dead body?

The Egyptians held that the heart, rather than the brain, was the most important organ. They considered it to be the source of all thoughts, feelings and intelligence. In fact, the heart was thought to testify for the dead person in the afterlife! This is why the Egyptians left the heart intact.

Q How were organs removed from the body?

The brain was pulled out through the nostrils with a metal hook and then thrown away. Other organs like the liver, lungs, stomach and intestines were usually removed by making an opening near the stomach, after which they were preserved in canopic jars.

Q Is it true that only the bodies of royal people were mummified?

At first, only Egyptian kings were mummified and buried inside royal pyramids. According to ancient legend, Osiris was the first Egyptian mummy. Later, common people also began to be mummified.

DAILY LIFE

The day-to-day life in ancient Egypt was not very different from the way people live today.

Family Values

The Egyptians highly valued their family life. They worked during the day and played games and listened to music in their free time. The father earned the livelihood, while the mother looked after the children and the home. The rich had servants to attend to the daily chores. People also kept pets such as cats and monkeys.

School Stories

Only rich families sent their boys to schools, which were called "houses of instruction". There they were taught by the learned scribes. They used papyrus paper, reed brushes and ink made from black soot and water. Girls did not go to school, but learnt music, dancing and household skills at home.

Egyptian students were taught hieroglyphs as well as mathematics and record-keeping. They wrote on ostraca (pieces of pottery) because papyrus was too costly to practice on

DAILY LIFE

What was the *shaduf*?

The *shaduf* was an irrigation device invented by the Egyptians for lifting water. It was made up of a long pole, which was held steady by a post stuck upright into the ground. A weight and a bucket hung from either end of the pole. The bucket would be lowered down to the water and lifted back with the help of the weight. By turning the pole, the bucket was then emptied into an irrigation channel.

The hand-operated shaduf was one of the earliest devices invented for water irrigation

The economy of ancient Egypt was largely based on farming, and the people spent much of their time on farming activities

Were the ancient Egyptians bald?

Most ancient Egyptians, both men and women, had their hair shaven regularly, and wore wigs instead! These wigs, made of human hair or sheep's wool, kept the shaved heads both warm and free from lice. The priests even shaved their entire bodies as further safeguard against lice!

Were houses in ancient Egypt decorated indoors?

The houses of rich Egyptian families had decorative wall paintings, coloured ceilings and tiled floors. Poorer homes were simple, with floors of beaten earth and hardly any decoration.

Was farming a major activity in ancient Egypt?

The economy of ancient Egypt was based on farming. Most of the people were farmers, and they spent a large part of the year raising cattle and growing crops. Part of these crops was given to the pharaoh as tax.

Did people in ancient Egypt wear make-up?

Both men and women in ancient Egypt took great care of their personal appearance, and wore a variety of make-up. They painted their eyes, lips and cheeks, using cosmetics made from natural, coloured minerals mixed with water and oil.

How important was the Nile River to the ancient Egyptians?

Most ancient Egyptians lived along the Nile, which provided them with water for drinking, bathing and agriculture. People transported crops, cattle and building materials in boats and barges on the Nile.

What kind of tools did farmers in ancient Egypt use?

Ancient Egyptian farmers used hand tools like the hoe, plough, sickle, fork and scoop. Later, the *shaduf* and the waterwheel were used to irrigate the crops.

The Egyptians wove sandals made of the reed plant

DAILY LIFE

 Did the ancient Egyptians buy things with money?

In ancient Egypt, people got their goods through exchange, instead of buying them with money. This was called barter. Goods were weighed on scales and exchanged with grains amounting to either the same weight or value.

 What kind of clothes was common in ancient Egypt?

The usual clothing for men was a loincloth or a kilt, while that for women was a simple dress held with straps. Royal and important people wore beaded dresses and decorative robes made of high-quality linen.

 How did ancient Egyptians clean their homes?

Ancient Egyptians usually cleaned their houses with brushes made of natural materials like tree fibres and reed.

The ancient Egyptians used grass and reed brooms

 Did the Egyptians use pillows?

In ancient Egypt, people did not use pillows. Instead, they used wooden or stone headrests. These were U-shaped supports believed to have been covered with cloth for cushioning.

 What kind of houses did the ancient Egyptians live in?

Most people in ancient Egypt lived in adobe houses. These were made of sun-baked mud bricks, straws and pebbles. The poor lived in single-room homes. The better-off classes had double-storey houses with at least two or three rooms. The rich homes had as many as 10 rooms.

Most people in ancient Egypt led simple lives in their adobe homes. They slept on wooden cots and headrests. The women looked after the house, baked bread, and groomed themselves, while the children played with toys

ARTS AND CRAFTS

Did you know that there was no specific word for "artist" in the ancient Egyptian language? Even so, art played an important role in everything, from religious duties to daily activities.

The Skilled Ones

Egyptian craftsmen usually learned their skills from their fathers. They were well-respected in society. Religious objects, made for temples and pharaohs, were made in special workshops inside the temple or the royal palace. Other items were crafted at smaller workshops.

Creative Crafts

Potters shaped vessels by hand and glazed them, before hardening them in fire. Goldsmiths crafted artistic jewellery, daily objects, statues and coffins, while sculptors carved beautiful statues, artefacts and monuments.

The skilled Egyptian sculptors carved statues to honor kings and queens, decorated temple walls, and crafted artefacts and other daily objects

ARTS AND CRAFTS

The throne of King Tutankhamun was found in his tomb by Howard Carter in 1922

Q Were the thrones of Egyptian pharaohs richly decorated?

The thrones of Egyptian pharaohs were usually crafted with precious metals and stones. King Tutankhamun's throne was made of wood and coated with pure gold. It was inlaid with a blue stone called faience and other semi-precious stones.

Q What kind of art was created in ancient Egypt?

Arts and crafts in ancient Egypt included textile and fibre weaving, tent making, papyrus craft, metal and stone sculpting, jewellery making and wall painting.

Q Which metals did Egyptian craftsmen use to make jewellery?

Egyptian craftsmen used copper and gold to make jewellery as well as statues. These were the earliest metals found in ancient Egypt. Excavated tombs from that time have revealed exquisite gold earrings, necklaces and neck collars.

These gold earrings, depicting birds with heads of ducks and wings of falcons, belonged to King Tut

Q What was the main purpose of art in ancient Egypt?

The ancient Egyptians usually created art for religious rituals. All forms of Egyptian art had special meaning and role in religion as well as for the afterlife.

The Egyptians believed that wearing amulets and charms on their jewellery would protect them from evil

Q What kind of decoration was often seen on ancient Egyptian jewellery?

Ancient Egyptian jewellery was often decorated with amulets. The people of ancient Egypt strongly believed in charms, so they wore bangles, necklaces and rings with amulet designs.

How were clothes made in ancient Egypt?

Clothes were made by weaving linen threads produced from the fibre of the flax plant. Usually women worked on the spinning looms.

Weaving in ancient Egypt was done mainly on hand-operated looms

Intricately carved ivory combs were often placed inside the tombs of royal mummies

Which well-known technique related to pottery was invented by the ancient Egyptians?

The art of coating pottery with enamel was invented in ancient Egypt. Sculptors used hand-operated potter's wheels to make clay dishes, which were used for cooking, eating, drinking and storing things.

ARTS AND CRAFTS

 What kind of tools did ancient Egyptian craftsmen use?

Ancient Egyptian artists used many different tools of stone, wood and metal. These included saws, bow drills, axes, chisels, awls, adzes, winnowing fans and sickles. The ostraca, a tool made from bits of pottery, was commonly used as pads for draft sketches.

 Did artists have rules for using different colours based on gender?

There were strict rules for using colours. Artists used only reddish-brown shades for colouring men's skin. Women figures were coloured in shades of yellow, and at times in pink too!

 Why were sculptures placed inside tombs?

Sculptures of all types and sizes were placed inside the tombs of the dead in ancient Egypt. Sculptures were seen as homes for the mummy's spirit, or gifts to a deity.

 Where did ancient Egyptian painters get their colours from?

Egyptian artists made their own colours by grinding natural materials like mineral rocks. Commonly used colours included black, white, grey, red, blue, green, pink and yellow.

 Why did ancient Egyptian artists paint the walls of tombs?

The Egyptians believed that paintings and relief images on tomb walls assured the dead person's survival in the afterlife. They often showed scenes from the life of the dead person.

One of the most important jobs of ancient Egyptian artists was painting the walls of royal tombs

ARCHITECTURE

Ancient Egyptian architecture, too, was influenced by religion. This is why the most elaborate structures were the temples and the pyramids.

Princely Pyramids

The Egyptians built pyramids to bury their pharaohs. Initially, single-level, square-shaped tombs (mastabas) were built, with just enough room for the coffin.

Later, the Egyptians built a series of steps on top of the mastabas, leading up to a flat-topped platform. These were the first proper pyramids, and were called step pyramids. The steps were believed to guide the dead to the heavens.

Still later, the steps were filled in to smoothen the sides. The Egyptians thought that the sunrays would reflect off the smooth sides to form a ramp leading to heaven! The most famous of these cone-shaped pyramids are the three Pyramids of Giza. One of these, the Khufu Pyramid, is the oldest standing structure among the Seven Wonders of the World! It was built for King Khufu over 4,000 years ago,

The earliest mastabas were made of mud brick, while the later ones were of stone, or stone-covered clay bricks

ARCHITECTURE

Which kind of architectural column was common in ancient Egypt?

Columns depicting the image of Hathor on the capital were commonly used in ancient Egyptian architecture. These columns were decorated with the sculpted head of Hathor, the goddess of love, joy and motherhood.

Columns featured prominently in the architecture of Egyptian temples

Ancient Egyptians used basic tools to cut, carve and shape building materials

What kind of tools was used to construct pyramids and temples?

The Egyptians used a number of tools for building pyramids and temples. Granite hammers, metal chisels, pickaxes and other strong tools were used to cut and carve hard stone blocks. Right angles and plumb lines were used to ensure that the sides of the stone blocks were in a straight line.

Which Egyptian temple was so designed that the statue inside could be lit up by the sun?

The gigantic Temple of Ramses II at Abu Simbel, which houses a big statue of Ramses II, was so designed that the sunrays could enter the inner sanctuary twice a year and light up the statue.

Were Egyptian temples made to look like plants?

The pillars and columns of Egyptian temples were often carved to look like palm trees, papyrus reeds and lotus plants.

The Great Pyramid of Giza is among the Seven Wonders of the Ancient World

Which was the first pyramid built in ancient Egypt?

The first known Egyptian pyramid was the Step Pyramid of King Zoser (Djoser), at Saqqara. Built nearly 5,000 years ago by the architect Imhotep, it was the biggest stone structure of its time.

How many people were needed to build a single pyramid?

Thousands of workers and artists were involved in the construction of a single pyramid. This often included more than 4,000 craftsmen and stonemasons, as well as farmers who worked mainly so that they could pay off their taxes.

Which is the largest stone structure in the world?

The Great Pyramid at Giza is the world's largest stone structure. Nearly 140 m (459 feet) tall, it is made up of more than 2 million blocks of limestone! The pyramid is famous for the massive Great Sphinx statue that guards it. It is believed to be amongst the largest sculptures ever.

FACT BOX

■ Imhotep of Egypt is considered to be the first known architect. He had built the complex of King Netjerikhet (Djoser) at Saqqara.

■ Pyramid workers commonly carried water bottles made of animal hide.

A water container made from animal hide

■ There are over 90 pyramids in Egypt. The last one was built in 1570 B.C. Pyramids were found to be easily accessible to robbers. From the New Kingdom onwards, pharaohs and their treasures were buried in tombs carved in cliffs, which lied hidden in a valley.

ARCHITECTURE

 Did workers actually lift stone blocks while building pyramids?

Pyramid workers could not have lifted such heavy blocks of stone on their own. Historians believe that sloping ramps were erected around the sides of the pyramid, somewhat like a stairway. The stone blocks were then placed on wooden sledges and pulled up the ramps by ropes.

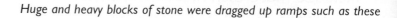

Huge and heavy blocks of stone were dragged up ramps such as these

 Why did the Egyptians build pyramids only on the west bank of the Nile River?

Since the sun set on the west bank of the Nile, the ancient Egyptians believed that this was the "land of the dead". They, therefore, built the pyramids on the west bank, while building their own houses on the east bank, the point of sunrise.

Were buildings and structures in ancient Egypt decorative?

In ancient Egypt, pyramids, palaces and temples were decorated with rich hieroglyphics, drawings and paintings. Hieroglyphs ("sacred carvings") were commonly used to carve pictures on walls. of temples and pyramids.

What materials were the pyramids of ancient Egypt made of?

Pyramids were built with massive slabs of different stones. Rough limestone was used for the main structure, while a finer, white limestone was used for casing the outer layer as well as the inner walls. Often, pink granite covered the walls inside. Basalt and alabaster were occasionally used for the floors.

 What role did the stars play in the building of Egyptian pyramids?

The ancient Egyptians built their pyramids and temples according to the pattern of stars in the sky. They used astrological tools like the *merkhet* ("instrument of knowing") to do this. Made from the rib of a palm tree leaf, the merkhet is said to be the earliest astronomical tool in the world.

GAMES AND ENTERTAINMENT

The people of ancient Egypt found different ways to entertain themselves in their free time.

Sporting Spirit

It is believed that the ancient Egyptians invented the sport of fencing (performed with blunt swords). Tomb drawings have also shown people playing with sticks made of palm-tree branches that resemble hockey sticks and a ball made of papyrus fibres. The Egyptians devised proper rules for their games, and even had referees, player uniforms and prizes!

Popular sports included running, swimming, wrestling, weightlifting, boxing, archery and rowing. Many of these were practiced for fitness.

Huntsman's Instinct

Egyptian men enjoyed hunting. Pharaohs held hunting to be a symbol of bravery. Hunting was also a way of getting meat for food. Animal bones, feathers, horns, leather and shells were used to make such items as clothes, jewellery and religious objects.

This stick-and-ball game played in ancient Egypt closely resembled the modern sport of hockey

GAMES AND ENTERTAINMENT

The very popular game of senet was played by both the rich and the poor

Which popular game played in ancient Egypt resembled the game of chess?

Senet was the national game in ancient Egypt for about 3,000 years. It was a board game played by both royal and common people, and was somewhat like chess and backgammon. The objective of the two-player game was to move all the counters across 30 squares on the board to reach the last square and then remove them.

Q Which ancient Egyptian game was named after two types of animals?

An ancient Egyptian board game called "Dogs and Jackals" featured four animal legs and a palm tree with about 55 holes carved on it. The game consisted of five counters for each player, with three coins that determined the movement of these counters. The person who first managed to move all his counters up the palm tree was the winner.

Q What was the "Tug of Hoop"?

The "Tug of Hoop" was a game played in ancient Egypt. Two people competed by pulling a common hoop towards themselves with a hooked stick. The players were not allowed to let the hoop fall flat on to the ground.

Music and dance were integral to any occasion or festival in ancient Egypt

Q How did ancient Egyptian children amuse hemselves?

Children in ancient Egypt played games like leap frog, hopscotch and goose step. Ball games were another popular pastime. Children also played with different kinds of toys.

Children in ancient Egypt played outdoor games like "khuzza lawiizza" (leap frog), tug of war, handball and wrestling

34

How was the ancient Egyptian sport of high jumping played?

Two people sat facing each other and stretched their legs out to create a jumping barrier. A third person had to jump over the barrier. The barrier could be increased by putting their palms over their feet. The third player would then attempt to jump without touching the barrier! The game is still played in parts of Egypt, and is known as "goose steps".

What kind of musical instruments were played in ancient Egypt?

The ancient Egyptians played string instruments like harps and lyres, wind instruments such as clarinets, flutes, oboes and lutes, and percussions like drums, tambourines and cymbals.

Who danced and played music at festivals and banquets?

Women from poorer families in ancient Egypt usually danced or played at important festivals and banquets.

FACT BOX

■ The Dancer of the Muu was a special dance performed by men during ancient Egyptian funerals. The dancers wore headdresses made of reeds.

■ The sistrum was an ancient Egyptian musical rattle. It was often played by women musicians in temples. Its sound was said to drive away evil powers!

A set of rings on the sacred sistrum created a rattling sound against metal crossbars

■ It is believed that the first form of the musical pipe organ was invented in ancient Egypt.

GAMES AND ENTERTAINMENT

 Were the ancient Egyptians good at gymnastics?

Ancient Egyptian gymnasts were skilled at performing complicated moves. Take the consecutive vault, for instance. This involved turning in mid-air more than once, without touching their heads on the ground! When finished, they would land to stand absolutely straight, which is still a gymnastics rule in the modern Olympics.

The Egyptians performed gymnastic exercises to keep themselves fit and strong

 Is the oldest document of sports recorded in Egypt?

The oldest document relating to sports is in the form of a mural painting in ancient Egypt. It shows the great pharaoh, Zoser the Great, participating in a running event during the Heb Sed Festival.

The Egyptians used nets, hooks and harpoons to catch fish. The earliest hooks were made out of animal bones, but later, metal hooks were used

Was the earliest record of bowling really discovered in Egypt?

The very first record of bowling has been dated to ancient Egypt, some 7,000 years back. A round object resembling the modern bowling ball and long marble bars that looked like bowling pins were discovered inside an ancient pyramid ruin.

Did people in ancient Egypt have feasts and festivals?

The ancient Egyptians held a variety of feasts and festivals. Festivals were usually celebrated for religious purposes, in honour of the gods and goddesses. The greatest number of festivals took place during the flood season.

 How do we know that the ancient Egyptians practiced fishing?

In ancient Egypt, fishing was a sport as well as a means of livelihood. Drawings on tomb walls show fishing scenes that inform us how people caught and consumed fish.

WOMEN IN ANCIENT EGYPT

It is said that women in ancient Egypt were very liberated for their time. They were more powerful than the women in any other ancient civilisation.

Equal Egyptians

Ancient Egyptian women enjoyed many of the same rights as men did. For instance, they were allowed to own, buy, sell and inherit land.

While most women stayed at home to look after their children, a few did jobs. Most worked as weavers, maids, nurses, gardeners, singers and dancers. Women from richer families were even known to become doctors and high priestesses!

Female Pharaohs

The most famous of Egypt's queens include Hatshepsut, Nefertiti and Cleopatra. Cleopatra, who became queen at the age of 18, was known for her intelligence and ambition.

Women from rich homes spent the day grooming themselves and playing with their children

EXTRAORDINARY EGYPT!

Q **How much gold jewellery was found inside King Tutankhamun's tomb?**

More than 5,000 articles of gold jewellery were discovered inside King Tut's tomb. The boy-king's mummified body itself contained nearly 150 pieces of gold jewellery. In addition, there were gold finger covers, necklaces, collars and rings. A falcon-headed collar found on the mummy was made up of about 250 pieces of gold!

The rich gold collar of King Tutankhamun

Q **What did people in ancient Egypt use for mixing cosmetics?**

The ancient Egyptian people used cosmetic spoons and palettes to mix colours, oils and ointments. The spoons were often in the shape of a female figure.

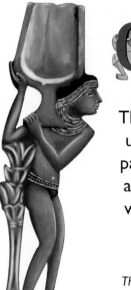

The Egyptians mixed and applied make-up with decorative cosmetic spoons of wood or metal

Q **How did the ancient Egyptians shave?**

Tomb excavations have revealed that the ancient Egyptians used both gold and copper razors to shave. The razors, dating back to the 4th Century B.C., were usually kept inside leather cases.

The ancient Egyptian doctors were much advanced for their time. They treated injuries and cured illnesses with the use of natural oils and plant extracts. Honey was commonly used to treat wounds

Q **Did the ancient Egyptians have a name for their parties?**

Any party held in ancient Egypt was referred to as a "house of beer"!

Q **How did the ancient Egyptians remove infections from the ear?**

The ancient Egyptians invented a method called "ear candling" to remove infections from the ear. They inserted one end of a cone-shaped, hollow candle into the ear cavity, and then lighted the other end. The smoke from the candle pulled out all the extra wax and germs from the ear!

38

What did ancient Egyptian pyramid workers eat for strength?

Workmen at pyramid sites were made to eat onions for strength! The ancient Egyptians believed that vegetables such as onion and garlic were good for health.

How did Egyptian doctors maintain hygiene while treating injuries and wounds?

Egyptian doctors understood the importance of hygiene, and disinfected their hands and surgical tools before treating anyone. They soaked bandages and plasters with herbs to quicken the healing process.

FACT BOX

■ It is believed that ancient Egyptian surgeons had their hands cut off if a patient of high status died during surgery!

■ The earliest references to the use of eye make-up date back to ancient Egypt. Both men and women painted their eyes with kohl – an eyeliner meant to make their eyes look bigger as well as to protect themselves from evil. Kohl was usually stored in long, decorative tubes and small pots.

Small and thin sticks were dipped into the cylindrical tubes to apply kohl on the eyes

■ Although the Egyptians invented glass, mirrors in ancient Egypt were not made of glass. The Egyptians did not know how to make clear glass. So they used such metals as polished bronze and silver.

EXTRAORDINARY EGYPT!

 Is the world's oldest bakery situated in ancient Egypt?

In the year 2002, what is believed to be the oldest bakery in the world was discovered at Giza. The bakery, which is over 4,000 years old, showed that the ancient Egyptians baked bread in large, bell-shaped pots called *bedjas*.

 How did the ancient Egyptians make perfume?

Egyptian perfumes were made from plant roots, leaves and flowers. Extracts from henna, cinnamon, iris, rose, lily and almond were soaked in either turpentine oil or animal fats, and sometimes even cooked!

The Egyptians made perfume flasks to carry and store oils and perfumes

 What did ancient Egyptian warriors wear?

Common soldiers in ancient Egypt wore white linen kilts, leather footwear and white headdresses. They carried bows and arrows. Pharaohs, who also often fought wars, wore colourful clothes and headdresses.

 What did people in ancient Egypt do if their cats died?

It is believed that people in ancient Egypt would shave their eyebrows in order to mourn the deaths of their cats!

In ancient Egypt, kings and soldiers often fought battles together

 Why did the ancient Egyptians place cones on top of their heads?

People in ancient Egypt often attached a cone of wax or animal fat to their heads and wigs. The cone was perfumed with herbs and spices. As it gradually melted, the perfume on it would spread all over the person's body and clothes!

INVENTIONS AND DISCOVERIES

Ancient Egypt was the birthplace of amazing discoveries in various fields, including science, medicine, mathematics, language and writing. Perhaps this is why it is referred to as the "cradle of civilisation"!

Time Tales

It was the Egyptians who discovered timekeeping. They kept track of time with upright stone columns called Cleopatra Needles. The Egyptians divided the day into 12 parts, which were represented by 12 marks on the ground. As sunlight progressed during the day, the length of the column's shadow changed. The shadow's length and position on the ground showed how much daylight, or time, was left!

Medical Magic!

The Egyptian physicians were among the first to use anaesthesia. They could also fix damaged faces by using artificial noses and ears! The Egyptians had also uncovered the healing powers of flowers, herbs and animals for treating injuries and infections.

This ancient Egyptian obelisk was shifted to London, England, in 1819

INVENTIONS AND DISCOVERIES

 Was bread invented in ancient Egypt?

The ancient Egyptians are widely believed to have invented leavened (raised) bread, which was also their most common food. Dried grains such as wheat or barley were baked in clay ovens to make loaves of bread. Pharaohs and priests had bread made with fruit and honey. It is said that during the New Kingdom, there were about 40 different types of bread!

 Was the first type of paper invented in ancient Egypt?

The first form of paper was created in ancient Egypt. Sometime in 4000 B.C., the Egyptians invented writing sheets from a river plant called papyrus, which served as a strong parchment. In fact, the word "paper" comes from "papyrus".

Priests and pharmacists process and record the techniques of

How did the ancient Egyptians contribute to the field of medicine?

The Egyptians uncovered the causes of various diseases and developed medicinal cures for them. The first medical documents are said to be the *Ebers Papyrus*, which recorded ways to make over 800 cures.

Which drink did the ancient Egyptians invent?

The ancient Egyptians invented beer. They made it from the crumbs of lightly baked bread loaves. The crumbs were soaked in water, and the mixture was fermented in huge containers to produce beer.

Beer was the most common drink in ancient Egypt. It is believed that the Egyptians flavoured their beer with date juice and honey!

Did the ancient Egyptians practice navel piercing?

The ancient Egyptians are said to have been the first people to pierce their belly buttons! However, only people of royal or important origin are believed to have been allowed to wear jewellery on the navel. If the common people went against the rule, they were supposedly punished with death.

Was the ancient Egyptian calendar any different from the modern one?

The ancient Egyptians were the first to devise the 365-day calendar. It consisted of 12 months and 3 seasons. However, a week was made up of 10 days, while a month had just 3 weeks! The last five days in the year were observed as the birthdays of their deities, namely Osiris, Horus, Seth, Isis and Nephthys.

How did the ancient Egyptians make paper from the papyrus plant?

Sheets of the papyrus plant's root were first soaked in water. These were then pressed together and dried. The sap inside the roots stuck the sheets together, creating a flat and strong writing surface.

FACT BOX

■ It is said that the toothpaste was invented in ancient Egypt over 4,000 years ago. The Egyptians mixed crushed pumice stone and vinegar to make their special tooth-cleaning paste.

■ It is believed that the Egyptians invented the mathematical concepts of geometry, trigonometry and algebra.

■ The ancient Egyptians kept bees for making honey. Images on tomb walls show that bee-keeping was practiced in Egypt as early as 2600 B.C. The people found that honey was good for healing as well as protecting and strengthening the body.

Egyptians used honey as food, as flavouring ingredient, in making perfume, and for treating wounds

INVENTIONS AND DISCOVERIES

Q **Was mosaic glass founded in ancient Egypt?**

The Egyptians invented the mosaic glass by fusing together pieces of coloured glass. This art form first appeared in Egypt about 1400 B.C.

Glass was invented by the ancient Egyptians over 9,000 years ago

Q **What is the ancient Egyptian system of writing called?**

The ancient Egyptian system of writing is known as hieroglyphics. The hieroglyphic script was developed about 3100 B.C. Instead of alphabets, hieroglyphics consisted of symbols called hieroglyphs, which symbolised different ideas and objects.

Q **What is significant about the toilet seats found in ancient Egypt?**

The first known toilet seat in the world was discovered in the ancient Egyptian city of Akhenaten in 1350 B.C. Ancient Egyptian toilet seats were said to be wooden, stone, or ceramic seats placed over huge bowls of sand!

The secrets of hieroglyphics were revealed to the world in 1799, with the discovery of the Rosetta Stone

Q **Did the ancient Egyptians invent the sailing boat?**

It is believed that the sail was invented in ancient Egypt. Dead people used to be sent to their burials by boat on the Nile. They were accompanied by mourners carrying poles with leather shields. Legend relates that in 3200 B.C., a mourner got tired of holding his pole, so he tied it to the funeral boat he was on. The boat began to sail when the wind blew, and the sail was born!

Q **Did the ancient Egyptians invent the potter's wheel?**

The earliest potter's wheel is said to have been developed by the Egyptian people during the Old Kingdom period. The device was a turntable that was turned round and round by hand.

The earliest form of the potter's wheel